WHERE DID POETRY COME FROM

SOME EARLY ENCOUNTERS } *Geoffrey O'Brien*

D1265188

MARSH HAWK PRESS | 2020

FIRST EDITION

1   3   5   7   9   10   8   6   4   2

Marsh Hawk Press books are published by Marsh Hawk Press, Inc.,

a not-for-profit corporation under section 501 (c)3 United States Internal Revenue Code

Library of Congress Cataloging-in-Publication Data

O'Brien, Geoffrey, 1948- author.

Where did poetry come from: some early encounters / Geoffrey O'Brien.

First edition. | East Rockaway, New York: Marsh Hawk Press, 2020.

LCCN 2019041213 | ISBN 9781732614116 (paperback)

O'Brien, Geoffrey, 1948—Childhood and youth. | O'Brien,

Geoffrey, 1948—Knowledge–Poetry. | Oral interpretation.

LCC PS3565.B6689 Z46 2020 | DDC 811/.54—dc23

LC record available at https://lccn.loc.gov/2019041213

Book design by Sandy McIntosh

Printed in the USA

Chapter One SERIES ❦ ON BECOMING A POET

Chapter One: On Becoming a Poet

The Chapter One Project from Marsh Hawk Press features the memoirs of outstanding poets

from diverse backgrounds recalling the ways by which they found their start as writers.

For more information about Chapter One, visit our Web site.

Marsh Hawk Press

P.O. Box 206, East Rockaway, NY 11518-0206

www.MarshHawkPress.org

for Star Black

What follows is not about wanting to be a poet

or trying to become a poet
or learning how to write
or forgetting how to write and starting over
or arguing about poetry
whether alone or with others
or attempting to come up with a valid general definition of
poetry
or even a valid private definition that would not dissolve and
change under pressure of constant unavoidable revision
only to be set aside finally as an always provisional cluster of
possibilities
tantalizing and radiant and unfinishable;
it is not about making a close study of leaves or waves or
constellations
or crouching to observe every species of natural transition and
every corresponding trope of mythical transmutation
or surveying the approximately infinite techniques of poem-
writing across time and space
or mastering the seven thousand types of ambiguity and
grammatical nuance
or delving to the root the etymology of any given word
or naming and ordering the varieties of cadence;
or pinpointing irreversible alterations in modes of expression
or savoring the internecine duels and denunciations of schools
and sects
or speculating how and when poetry emerged in the timetable of
human evolution or in the formation of primeval tribes or in the earliest
inscribing of epics or love songs or healing incantations.
The question here was only
where did poetry come from in a single random life,
a question permanently open like a vowel that finds no
consonants to give it form and duration and direction;
how did it make its presence known before it had been given a
name
what could have suggested that such a thing existed
what kind of suggestions were stumbled upon no matter how
loosely or crudely understood, if understood at all,
messily, partially, apprehended in side views, or by getting words
wrong as when hearing a song on the radio

imposing new meanings on words or phrases by whim or
compulsion;
    through what fitful chance encounters
    did a notion however blurred form out of shivers, scratches,
caresses, tremors and fits, intercepted repetitions, alluring patterns and
curious views, voices unknown even if intimately familiar people gave
utterance to them, seasons
    of baffling incomprehension
    experiences so unforgettable you are driven to make contact with
them again
    to discover you can make contact only by inventing them
    as in a memoir where only what is quoted is certifiably authentic
    the rest of it being a more or less fictional journey through
accumulated fragments, a few strips of rag that dangle in the mind like
weathered signposts, nudged into view by an aroma or breeze
    what sticks and clicks in the night tunnel, insistent drumbeats
and hiccups
    leading back to chamber or gulf or cavelike aperture or mad
ancestor's attic
    a spectral location disguised as memory of a first encounter.
    Where did poetry come from
    and is it still there
    continuing to spread outward beyond apprehending
    continuing to escape
    in the sound always present and never altogether sounded
    drifting up from beneath the temporary stopover where the
hearer only perches
    haunted like a house by what is overheard
    a transience perpetually surviving.

CONTENTS

1.

Diddle diddle dumpling
My son John

Went to bed
With his stockings on

One shoe off
And the other shoe on

Diddle diddle dumpling
My son John

A woman's voice is speaking it.

She knows what comes next. Her voice expresses the pleasure of knowing it. Anticipates your pleasure. Anticipates her own pleasure at being about to shape the sounds yet one more time.

The sounds were once uttered to her in the same fashion. By which utterance she was in part fashioned. As she now in turn is fashioning. A cycle becomes apparent to her in the rounded motion of it rolling in its grooves. Molding with molded sounds. Giving form to air. Counting out, as an accompaniment to touching, an extension of touching.

Contact.

The occasion of the rhyme is an infant's bedtime. It marks a transition. It masks an interruption. It distracts from the intrusion of being lifted out of play, hauled into the disagreeable discipline of having free movement restricted, of going through all the stages of washing and undressing and being put into bed and given over to darkness. A break point approaches. Soon the mouth of a cavern will swallow the room and all it holds.

A woman's voice. It could have been a man's voice but in memory never was. Not speaking but half chanting and half teasing. It is the sound of an intimate knowledge of the inside of the body. A sound of love or what sounds like love, of a desire to give comfort. Of the pleasure of sharing what is almost too silly to be said aloud. Of a holy and inane abandonment.

Diddle

What is diddle. What does diddle look like. Like nothing at all. It is the sound of some unsuspected capacity hidden in the mouth.

Diddle diddle

The action of the tongue moving back and forth against the top of the mouth. Just shy of where the teeth start. A ticklish repetition that could go on forever.

Dumpling

A round and busy sound, closing together and popping apart. Funny in itself and pleasurable to say again and again. A sound shaped like the mouth. And likewise a thing, something remembered and desired, a foodstuff *scrumptious,* word in which the texture of a dumpling in the mouth joins with the imagined flavor now permeating the sound of the word and the part the word plays in the rhythm of what is being put forth, in a place liberated from constraint and permanently surprising and pleasing. And somewhere inside it, on the reverse side of its syllables if you could follow them that far back, perhaps the surprise of having a body at all.

My son John

Three even claps. Whose son? Who's John? Who speaks? Another infant entering another bed. Everything has already happened before. In the place across the way, wherever that way might be, the way where the words have already been, the country where they went pioneering, in the rhyme where everything that long ago happened is happening again. It happened and so the words are shaped this way. Everything that happens now *must* happen because it already did. Is in movement and can no longer be stopped.

Went to bed
With his stockings on

Heard before understood. Memorized before understood. A picture formed without asking why or how. The ruts of its sounds familiar like floorboards many times crawled over. A story told before any sense of what a story was. Why did it happen. Was it shameful that it happened. So shameful or ridiculous or miraculous that a rhyme was made of it.

One shoe off

The clomp of a shoe falling to the floor. Hitting the floor on the last beat.

And the other shoe on

An answer coming back, from other to one. A dance taking place, tilting back and forth from off to on. As if seesawing in a basket. A basket of contradictions. One on, other off. Light off, night on.

Diddle diddle dumpling
My son John

The voice falling now not rising. The same words come back only to say that this time it's over—once was to open, twice to close—the utterance snaps shut, ending where it started, returned inside itself. Swaddled in night. Engulfed.

Finally it will rise again to the surface as an inner voice, if not the voice of the listener then a voice that installed itself within, reciting what never needed to be memorized. It nudged its way into memory, finding by stealth a place already established for it. Where it will now continue to repeat itself. Perhaps for the pleasure of it. Pleasure on the part of who or what. Living machinery that plays its own music to itself. In any event not to be evicted.

To be joined by so many others, they will rattle around together, rhymes with crumbs of stories in them, the tales of Mother Hubbard's poor dog and Peter the pumpkin eater and the woman in the gigantic shoe, the cadaverous husband and the enormous plump wife, of the mouse and the clock and the dish and the moon, of Jack and Jill and their disastrous fate at the bottom of hill. Not tales at all since you can never know anything further of them or what happened before or after, nothing actually of what any of this is about beyond its own grotesque fragmentary reality. Something simply was and was imprinted. The rhyme is proof of its finality.

Comforting because known, if for no other reason. Even if not chosen, somehow at home in a world of pails and shoes and barking dogs and water buckets. Of knocks and cracks and frights worn away into harmlessness, now merely odd, messages from beings who can say this and nothing more, which is like saying nothing. The same nothing over and over. Why did they fall? Who had ever known them?

Not tales but shreds of sound. Pieces of thump.

See saw Marjory Daw
Pease porridge in the pot
Some in rags and some in tags

Alive only in the satisfaction of the edge of the tongue hitting the spot. To make the sound come right, any obstacle having been taken out of the way. Passage made clear.

And the beat ever after to be heard underneath at the bottom of it

Ding dong bell
Full fathom five
Fee fi fo fum
Tweedledee and Tweedledum
Boomlay boomlay boomlay boom

Dark ocean floor.

2.

Robin Hood
Robin Hood
      Riding through the glen

Robin Hood
Robin Hood
      With his band of men

Feared by the bad
Loved by the good

Robin Hood
      Robin Hood
            Robin Hood

Television.

The theme breaks into the uninterrupted flow that is afternoon. To hear it at all you have to be aware of what time it is on the clock.

Time to hear the sound that will sound only once until next week. You may have to run from play in the yard to get there.

It is the summons to a beginning, the trumpet sounding before the joust, that finally will be the only thing remembered. It promised what endured only in the theme itself. All else, names and plots, bleached out to a crisscrossing shape as skeletal as the rafters of a barn. **Men** in a **glen**. **Feared** is to **bad** as **loved** is to **good**.

Compressing to four words

Riding through the glen

all of the story that counted. An eternal state of progressing through open space. All the happening that need ever happen.

The event is a picture. The picture is a sound. All are one. The past is now. The glen is here. The riding is continual within the words. Four words that are one word—glyph. Capsule or module in which you are transported. Without moving. Without actually going anywhere. Radiating in space. The movement itself motionless.

Four-word phrase within which nothing ever ends. Perpetual going-through.

Through what? A glen. What is a glen?

What is gone through. Compound of light and horse and rock and green. Of hill of grass. Of spur. Of air.

Eternal mystery of **glen**

3.

a little dab'll do ya

Say it over and over again.

       a little dab'll do ya
       a little dab'll do ya
       a little dab'll do ya

Sung over and over in high-pitched harmony.
Bryllcreem.
The words melt into one another making a form of curved space. Soft
glassy waves folding over and merging. Glossy tunneling weaves. All forms
of resistance having been smoothed into this other language.
Spell that must be spoken aloud to have power.

       abracadabra

Miracle.
Bryllcreem.

4.

dark brown is the river
        golden is the sand
it flows along forever
        with trees on either hand

green leaves a-floating
        castles of the foam
boats of mine a-boating
        where will all come home

on goes the river
        and out past the mill
away down the valley
        away down the hill

away down the river
        a hundred miles or more
other little children
        shall bring my boats ashore

THERE WERE PHRASES found in Robert Louis Stevenson that stuck like pictures in a book seen once and never after unseen, returned to out of need

my bed is a boat
I never can get back by day
the trees are crying aloud
all night across the dark we steer
to Providence or Babylon
shivering in my nakedness
see the spreading circles die
cities blazing in the fire

the terrors of night for once spoken aloud, the power of fires and shadows.
     And by morning light other words stood out

hayloft
meadow-side
wagons
mill wheel

made of straw and weathered wood, pictures of a scarcely known world. World continuous with sun and ground and hedge.
     In this book, handed down in an already crinkled copy, crayon marks in its margins, what was hidden was being revealed. A constant opening up. Nobody knew of these things except Robert Louis Stevenson. First named author. Secret voice, intimate presence.
     The words are places and in the middle of them—the middle of themselves—they want to move beyond into other places

I should like to rise and go
where the golden apples grow

and that is enough. The words can stop right there, stay forever on that rising note, suspended until they find themselves where everything has been all along, staring into water, the cool water always to be found lapping at the edge of the hiding place under some bridge, the edge of some clear stream

O the clean gravel!

A child makes boats out of paper. The boats are set floating in a stream and go out of sight and are lost. They are not lost. They will find a harbor among other children. Unknown children in an unknown world.

The children are not there. They are not to be seen. They are other. Who are they anyway. They are somewhere. On the other side. After the words end.

Where does poetry come from.

Where Go the Boats?

5.

'Twas brillig, and the slithy toves
    Did gyre and gimble in the wabe:
All mimsy were the borogroves,
    And the mome raths outgrabe.

Not having had such a long time to get accustomed to language yet already happy to sneak out. To get back to where perhaps something had been left behind. It was a woman's voice again—the visiting aunt whose voice by itself brought light into the house—reciting, from memory, with the air of someone sharing a great secret.

(When had she memorized it. How did she come to know it. She sounded the words as if they were made specially for her. In another century, long after everyone else in that house had died, blind and immobilized, she would still rejoice in reciting it from memory.)

And it was as if these creatures had been caught sight of—by an unearthly light—in a clearing that must certainly exist. It was there because it could be said aloud.

slithy toves

Not by any means quite like the ones in the book's illustration—with corkscrew snout or distended stick-legs—but shaped like the sound of the words. Consisting of nothing but that. And thereby having bodies. Waddling about slow and sidewise—huffing, slumping, wheezing, grumping—almost resistant to absorbing light into their leather-plated bodies—on a bank of some hidden river, an opening here named

the wabe

where they live their disconnected life. No subsequent explanation, not even Lewis Carroll's, could possibly live up to the delight and freedom of words that once set loose could not ever be sent into exile. They made places for themselves all the richer for being empty apertures, weird nests, having found a place to laze or burrow among the syllables of

mimsy
and **uffish**
and **vorpal**

—the words being window in what had otherwise been wall. To come to know a nonsense word was to know for the first time what a word was. Of course without the wall—the sentences within which the words acted their parts—there could be no windows either. But what relief to let air into the stifling enclosure of something having to mean something. As it rushed in, even the other words

thought
and **flame**
and **wood**

themselves betrayed signs of erosion, fault lines that might show them to be only partly solid. Somewhere in their core they were as **mimsy** as **borogroves**.

6.

For they're hangin' Danny Deever, you can hear the Dead
      March play,
The Regiment's in 'ollow square—they're hangin' him to-day;
They've taken of his buttons off an' cut his stripes away,
And they're hangin' Danny Deever in the mornin'.

He did a bad thing and they are hanging him.

A male voice this time. An older brother reciting with musical enthusiasm from a flaking leatherbound book, a cheap reprint on thin paper almost worn through with much reading. He performs in his bedroom for himself and anyone who can hear. Most of the words are incomprehensible but the rhythm is like a stampede and the refrain comes around inexorable and not to be forgotten

O they're hangin' Danny Deever in the mornin'!

once the necessary explanation has been made to his little brother ("they are hanging him because he did something bad") since to provide such explanations, the ones not all care to undertake, is part of his role. Of what it means to be hanged. What that does to the neck and the breath. How final it is. Here for the first time maybe, along with the first

Dead March

thudding into awareness. The harsh world took up its place with

bugles
and **bitter beer**

and the sergeant on hand

To turn you out, to turn you out

barking a deadly spell.

Soldiers had already been seen on parade in the warm weather on Memorial Day. There were pistols and pilot's goggles stored in closets as souvenirs of war, sergeant stripes and dog tags tucked in envelopes. Left right left. Bugle call. Day is done. Canvas smell of tents. Distant fear of uniforms, orders, drills. Rumored flag ceremonies of the Cub Scouts, at the time when all the boys were going to become Cub Scouts. The temptation of slinking away.

The soldier in terror asks what is happening and the sergeant tells him. In march time.

A ballad as the sound of the real. The **bitter** never yet tasted. A disaster forcing its way into permanent memory as if by means of a branding iron. Horror made song, become habit, an exercise of strength.

A rhythm to perk up the body even though

they're hangin' Danny Deever in the mornin'

7.

By the rivers of Babylon, there we sat down, yea, we wept, when we remembered Zion.

We hanged our harps upon the willows in the midst thereof.

For there they that carried us away captive required of us a song; and they that wasted us required of us mirth, saying, Sing us one of the songs of Zion.

How shall we sing the LORD's song in a strange land?

If I forget thee, Jerusalem, let my right hand forget her cunning.

A PLACE IS come upon, that never afterwards can go away. Suspended clearing at river's edge. Willows grow in its midst. Harps hang on them.

Out of the Sunday school stream of words recited, memorized, sung, repeated, the ear takes what it wants. **By the rivers of Babylon**—a location from that moment occupying real space and not to be budged—**there we sat down**—thereby, in answer to the place marked by two heavy beats, performing an action with two responding beats. The action was commanded by the place, a response inseparable from the fact of being there.

Geography and history born in twinned phrases. A birth taking place in the sounding of a cadence infinitely firm and flexible. A sea-like heave of words interwoven forever, emerging from the deepest source and still connected. Yet there and touchable—**willows** and **harps**—visitable almost. What was picture, what was sound? **Yea, we wept when we remembered Zion**. There could be a picture of tears on ancient cheeks. But no picture at all of **Zion**—hovering luminous nothingness akin to God or Eternity, words at whose center everything dissolves into bright unseeable core.

Words bound together more tightly than by rhymes, clotted together: **they that carried us away captive**. The words' edges press against each other, no gaps left between, bundled like captives. From that cluster **song** is pressed out—song they are ordered to sing—do they refuse? **How can I sing**. Being captives they must. This is the song, the refusal to sing.

Everything is taking place **in a strange land**—but it is all strange, the words themselves (the right hand is a girl and forgets **her** cunning), the existence of Babylon and Jerusalem, the taking of captives. (Just outside the window the sun shines on a parking lot.) Ancient weeping. Ancient singing. The Bible is what will not change. Black book with numbered sentences and words in another language, only ever allowing itself to be partly understood. Words burning black against the almost transparent paper. Exacting actions—bowed heads or muttered repetitions—a system of movements that the words in some way determine.

Psalm feels like a desperate movement from inside out, as if to throw yourself into the sky by voice alone. Moving toward a contact that seems finally to be with the words themselves, only that, coil of sound into which everything else is woven—must be woven—if anything is to be believed.

If the movement were not outward and upward it would crush you. Exhale it so as not to let it fall on you.

What moves outward is surge in which are carried

rivers   willows   harps   songs   Zion

rising like smoke from a sacrificial fire in the Bible illustration of a sheep brought to an altar.

There is a glistening **in the midst thereof** as if a moistening light seeped into the letters and became part of their substance.

The glistening hovers most perceptibly around certain phrases, certain sections. These can be detached from the rest, looked at without thinking of how they are connected to anything else. Follow the words along and you come at the end of it to where what began in the willows calls out to the **daughter of Babylon: Happy shall he be, that taketh and dasheth thy little ones against the stones**.

That final passage is marked as something to come back to in later days as if it were bracing to submit to an ancient shock of babies smashed against stone. Like an accident glimpsed once (despite being told not to look) from the window of a moving car. A violence not to be believed, a world so far from the Sunday School classroom with its sullen harmless calm, where God is constantly spoken of and not a thing ever happens. There are small quizzes, and ribbons given for regular attendance, inscribed with a "name verse" beginning with the first letter of one's name. None of the children seem ever to enjoy themselves there, or expect to. Any pleasures seem stolen, even from words come upon by accident. A boy slides his open Bible across with a mischievous grin, to point out the dirty bits in the Song of Solomon. The liveliest interest anyone showed. Otherwise waiting to get out in the air again, free and far from these words and even more from the flat expressionless tone in which they are read aloud.

8.

−thou rememberest

once I sat upon a promontory

and heard a mermaid on a dolphin's back
uttering   harmonious breath

−I remember

−flying between the cold moon and the earth
Cupid

a certain aim he took

but   Cupid's   shaft   passed on

it fell upon a little western flower
before milk-white, now purple with love's wound

A COMIC BOOK published in 1951, left lying in a pile of other comic books. *Stories by the World's Greatest Authors: A Midsummer Night's Dream.*

Flip through it looking at images, with no thought even of beginnings or endings—a winged elf-like being taking aim with a bow, a woman stabbing herself with a dagger held in both hands, a man with the head of a donkey, people in robes and sandals wandering in a wood and getting lost in fog, winged girls hovering in the air over a forest clearing, an arrow piercing a white flower now turned purple, and then once more the elf—his face isolated in a circular frame, with an expression neither happy nor sad—infant and wizened old man combined in one—but with the look of mysterious deep concentration: **I remember**.

To recognize and understand at first only that phrase, among the sprawl of words still opaque and resistant: **spheres, vestal, dote, leviathan,** even **promontory** (although here helpfully footnoted as "a big rock jutting out into the sea" and illustrated with Oberon and Puck at a distance, seated on dark rocks looking out toward ocean).

Returning how many times for the pictures and always circling back to those words

I remember

a point of contact sealed by the expression of Puck's face, haunting because indeterminable, even if the indeterminability may have been only a result of the illustrator's shortcomings: the accidental sublime. An ancient child whose memories are of other worlds, these pictured worlds of forest and mask and transformation. It took a long time, many turnings of the pages over months or was it years, to work outward from that point and take in what surrounded it. Slowly coming to feel that all this was and somehow is real, real as **cold moon** through backyard trees. Real as an **arrow** or a **flower**. An eerie secret.

Real because where else could it have come from? And how else could it have been recognizable?

It fell upon a little western flower

nothing easier to hold in the mind. What pleasure to find clearings where every word was simple. How is the beauty of this knowable. Where does its sorrow come from. An arrow hits a flower and turns it purple

with love's wound

—a wound like that of Thisby on the last page plunging a dagger into her breast—yet here nothing more than a purple flower surrounded by white flowers under the cold moon.

Here mysteries begin. Where do they end.

9.

They speak of seven sins in the Scripture
But our age has invented many more
So subtle and sweet that once you've slipped you're
Never never able to go home any more

Some can be bought for money
And some there are that glory can buy
  Some yield their purity
  In search of security
And some drown their dreams in a bottle of rye

Some go for empty knowledge
And some think sex will set their body free
  The man of the hour
  Will settle for power
Yes, every soul alive has his fee

UNKNOWN WORDS ARE everywhere but some repositories are particularly dense with them. The Bible. Shakespeare. A song of Gilbert and Sullivan was often a closet full of such terms and names—**quadratical, binomial, hypotenuse, animalculous, acrostics, paradox, Caradoc, Heliogabalus, Zoffanies, cuneiform, ravelin**—so many that the sheer profusion seemed a kind of magic trick, set to rhyme and music as they were, a dance of the incomprehensible making each word laughable.

Then there was *The Golden Apple*, a musical—a retelling of Homer set in turn of the century America—that came and went Off Broadway in 1954 and was preserved partially on an original cast album. Here in the lyrics of John Latouche are mingled the partly familiar and the partly exotic, questions for parents to answer and by their answers bring an earlier time into view: **moxie? Nick Carter? Japanese lanterns? no axe to grind? the vapors? bubbly on the ice? rock and rye? honky-tonk saloons?**

Or was the time not so much earlier. There are honky-tonk saloons or what look like them on movie posters and down the hill on the other side of the highway.

This must be still the language of the present world—of adults who drink martinis and have checkbooks—a terminology whose weight is already felt but whose precise value is still unknown—**money, purity, security, rye, sex, power, fee**. Every word heavy, and heavier when set knocking against other words. **Soul**—a Sunday School word for something not ever seen—has a **fee**. **Knowledge** can be **empty**. This had not been taught elsewhere. **Every soul alive** would include oneself.

The beat falls on **sex**—decisive drum accent—the word already separated out from others, loud and vague and known, without asking, to be heaviest: the name for what belongs to adults, even more than cigarettes and rye. The song makes a joke of it. All of it, that nighttime world, seems to be a joke here.

A song like a trailer at the movies for coming attractions. The glimmer, like that of a distant neon bar sign, of a sense that every fate has already been written down, by others.

10.

a strange city lying alone

shrines and palaces and towers

the melancholy waters

light from out the lurid sea

up fanes   up Babylon-like walls

stone flowers

that wilderness of glass

hideously serene

amid no earthly moans

Hell, rising from a thousand thrones

POE: A FIRST marker of fear. The comic book image of a woman's body thrust upward into a chimney by an escaped orangutan, or one-eyed man in nightcap staring at the long-haired intruder who is about to strangle him. Man in jester costume chained to a wall while another man seals him off with a barrier of bricks. Fear, and the irresistible need to return to the place of fear. Under the fear, cruelty. Under the cruelty, more fear.

Poe: "son of poverty-stricken actors… foster-father insisted that Edgar abandon all literary ambitions… reduced to direst poverty… dismissed for disgraceful conduct… financial panic… Poe continued to write… to no avail… his works were never accorded their proper valuation during his lifetime… stricken by inconsolable grief… took heavily to drink… won the antagonism of society for appearing arrogant and bad-hearted… found unconscious… died… alone and friendless." Comic book image of his head with radiant light behind it.

Poe: a book of stories with a vocabulary only partly, or not at all, understood—**fatality, metempsychosis, preternatural, estranged, Pyrrhonism**—and phrases suspended in some partly revealed space, hanging like ominous promises transcribed from lost books—**region of shadows, tumultuous and convulsive motion, each in the despairing posture of his fall, outcast of all outcasts, wild dominions of monastic thought, idolatrous Egypt, a mental sorcery long forgotten, too divinely precious not to be forbidden**—given comprehensible form by sudden savage acts of mutilation and blood-letting.

Poe: the one who had ventured into unknown places, far down in the sunken city. The City in the Sea: to be entered by reading it over and over. City made of what exactly? Of stone enclosures and ramparts—**turrets, towers, spires, domes, shrines, palaces, halls,** and the mysterious **fanes**—drowned interiors. Spaces made for play, miniature castles built out of blocks or pebbles, without any form of life but **flowers** and **ivy** carved in stone. The safest refuge, perfectly airless **wilderness of glass**, sealed up in itself in the aftermath of every possible disaster. The head peering down into the words as if through aquarium blur, submerged without ever running out of breath. A child's garden of **Hell** bright with **lurid sea** and **luminous waves** and a **redder glow** forcing its way out from what is buried under the words, to bring the structure **Down, down** like every toy castle. But it does not go away, it is still there preserved **hideously serene** in the beauty that Poe invented, or inhabited, or inherited but from whom.

Poe: an illustrated volume from a set by the Heritage Press. Its companions were by Emerson (a covered bridge, a patriotic statue, a mountain stream) and Whittier (snowbound farmland, a flag waved from a window). For Poe the black-and-white lithographs showed spectral women in white, ruined citadels, freakish tree-shapes glimmering with unnatural light, a bell tolling in a stone belfry, an animate skeleton looking down from a rocky ledge. From the window a view of robins darting across the grass. On the radio Perry Como singing *Catch a falling star and put it in your pocket*. Vacuum cleaner in an upstairs bedroom. Why not go play while the sun is out.

Poe: the necessary book, necessary because the words are stored and may be suddenly required. Consulted, like a book of spells.

11.

            The raven himself is hoarse
that croaks the fatal entrance of Duncan
under my battlements   Come you spirits
that tend on mortal thoughts   unsex me here
and fill me from the crown to the toe top-full
of direst cruelty

            Come thick night
and pall thee in the dunnest smoke of Hell
that my keen knife see not the wound it makes
nor Heaven peep through the blanket of the dark
to cry   Hold, hold!

THE RECORDED VOICE of Pamela Brown as Lady Macbeth is dark velvet, each word sounded with love and urgency, a sonorous clarity as of a French horn penetrating **thick night** and **dunnest smoke**. Dark music of a lullaby too gently coaxing to be resisted—a caress—a recording played repeatedly so as to be in the presence of that voice, rapt with the enchantment of what it utters.

This was the same Lady Macbeth who in the comic book version was a twin of Sleeping Beauty's stepmother, the same dark-haired murderess, luring her husband into cruel murder.

Now, in the realm of phonographic recording where nothing exists but sound, she speaks from the heart of a wise knowing, as if she inhabited a future where everything has already come to pass—the raven has already croaked—and she is aware of every detail, every hesitation, every hidden thought, every unspoken outcry. A world where nothing is but terror—and who would have thought it could be so beautiful. Beauty that has a hook in it, that drags along a lingering inward ache, the pain of what cannot ever be erased, the thought that must be listened to and acted on. Irresistible temptation to be carried beyond known limits to find what is there.

A violence felt but not well understood—**Unsex me**—sounds like a severing of language—or of body—both at once—a spell like those of witches. Take the body out of itself.

And other violence too visible to be pushed away from memory:

> **I have given suck, and know**
> **How tender 'tis to love the babe that milks me:**
> **I would, while it was smiling in my face,**
> **Have pluck'd my nipple from his boneless gums,**
> **And dash'd the brains out…**

like the Babylonian infants against the stones in the book of psalms. A history of smashed bodies hidden under all of it, unknown only because not yet revealed. Beginning to poke out from under. At first there is always the shudder of not wanting to hear, or even imagine. Not wanting to understand the necessity of this destructive intrusion.

Waking in the middle of the night—under a blanket in **the blanket of the dark** without any deeper hiding place—to thoughts that cannot be evaded. Unable to be anything but what in that moment you find yourself to be. Frightened of being frightened. Frightened of being like Macbeth—

stars, hide your fires
let not light see my black and deep desires

—frightened of the light that will shine on concealed thought.

How frightened could Macbeth be, him (in the comic book) a brawny bearded warrior in helmet and fur cape, a worthy companion for Kirk Douglas in *The Vikings*?

The warrior begins to fall apart into his words. He and his Lady pace halls of sounds, echoing rooms of audible thoughts. They walk up and down in lines that are like battlements, accompanied, as on the recording, by rains and gale-force winds. Smoky realm of words pierced with fiery glimmers, and with blood gushing out, lit by flashing images of breasts dripping gall and babies' brains dashed against stone. Language constantly interrupted by pictures. The language that plays in the dark when not sleeping, while the unwanted thoughts impose themselves.

The sounds themselves are the place where they are spoken. The walls are made from reverberating syllables.

Words that have the beauty of what will not allow itself to be forgotten. However one might wish it to be. The more deeply hidden the more beautiful. The more painfully brought forth the more remembered.

In saying it aloud Lady Macbeth enjoys the freedom that can be heard in Pamela Brown's voice. Her relief—joy—at letting everything out into the world with no more fear of consequence. Could this possibly be the sound of evil. Anything would be better than to cower in hiding. Her husband trembles and stammers, a bundle of nervous hesitations and wobbling arguments with himself, is **green and pale** but she almost serene in her sureness—**Leave all the rest to me**—like a mother with a frightened child. Unbearable to be in his situation. Anything would be better than to waver, or to be inwardly at war, to shrink from acting on compulsive desire, even if

it will make us mad

but by then everything will already be over. Fully unfolded out of the dark wherein it was born.

12.

How beautiful is the Princess Salome tonight!

Look at the moon. How strange the moon seems! She is like a woman rising from the tomb. She is like a dead woman. One might fancy she was looking for dead things.

She has a strange look. She is like a little princess who wears a yellow veil, and whose feet are of silver. She is like a princess who has little white doves for feet. One might fancy she was dancing.

Like the Bible, but not.

Full of pictures like psalms are. The moon. The princess. The moon is the princess. Looking for dead things. Dancing.

Like the Bible made strange.

Close to the Bible, curiously close, inhabiting the same places, with the same people in them: Salome, Herod, John the Baptist, Pharisees, Nazarenes. And speaking in an echo of the same rhythms.

But unfolding on a great terrace where a sophisticated party is being given, wine is being served, and the pointed conversation never stops—**The gods of my country are very fond of blood—In my country there are no gods left**.

As if it were part of some other Bible that partly overlaps. Where hitherto unfamiliar whispers are overheard.

What is said is constantly surprising and there is no way not to keep on reading. The rhythm insists, the back-and-forth saying the same things slightly differently—**You are always looking at her. You look at her too much—He is looking at something.—He is looking at someone—You must not look at her. You look too much at her.—Why do you look at her? You must not look at her**—each time nudging the movement forward, never allowing a pause where you could pull back, move aside, tear yourself way from eavesdropping, stop trying to steal a glimpse of what is happening in the adjacent banqueting hall. It is all one piece, spoken in different voices, but one continuous piece, a space that pulls the outsider— the spy—the child—into it. A secret theater, secret recitation.

No one has said this is a forbidden book—it is an ornamental volume with decorative illustrations in the margins of every page—but the adjectives announce it themselves—**forbidden—terrible—poisonous— defiled—abandoned—hideous—loathsome—horrible—mad— drunken—sick—pale**.

This then must be the poisonous Bible, the sick Bible. But beautiful. With **feet of silver, a white rose, doves that fly to their dove-cots, white butterflies**: says the voice of the one who must soon stab himself because he cannot bear to go on seeing and hearing.

Beautiful and dead, beautiful and poisonous, beautiful and sick: **a crime against some unknown God**.

But always to be begun, again, gone through to the end, all the while all the words were imprinting themselves, in the light cast on them by the torches of this particular night-time terrace: **eyelids, scarlet, ivory, censer,**

music, blasphemies, athirst, passion, virgin, veins, mystery, Death.

Associations twining around themselves, like decorative ivy embossed on a goblet.

The introduction to the Heritage Press edition of *Salome* provided an assurance: "Art purifies all subjects, not by idealizing them but by showing them in true relation to life."

13.

This is it; this Lemnos and its beach
down to the sea that quite surrounds it; desolate,
no one sets foot on it; there are no houses...

Look about
and see where there might be a cave with two mouths.

THERE ARE ARCHEOLOGICAL ruins where people once spoke. The sites of lost civilizations. Photographs can be found in magazines and books. Stone columns with pine trees and ocean visible in the spaces between them. Blue sky. No people. Ancient empty paradise.

Here were gods of every kind: transparent, volcanic, naked, magical, destructive, protective. Living in trees and ponds; traveling into clouds; capable of entering anywhere; capable of sending dreams, killing, playing music, delivering secret messages, changing people into spiders and flowers and stars. Weblike perpetually changeable world of gods. As if their home were underwater, or inside a cloud.

All gone.

In place of that, rock fragments and sea wind. Sun.

The fascination of the Greek play of *Philoctetes*—where a wounded Greek whose foul-smelling wound made his comrades abandon him on an island was now to be brought back by Odysseus and the son of Achilles, to help them win the Trojan War—was what wasn't there. The emptiness of the island. Two people arriving from the sea to find another person who doesn't want to be found. All around them only rock and air and sea.

This is it—

just that—

beach—desolate—no houses—cave.

All that is not lost, cannot be lost because already isolated and abandoned. No decorations on any of it, no furniture. The man alone there with nothing to think but

Hateful life, why should I still be alive and seeing?
Why not be gone into the dark?

almost comforted by having nowhere else to go, nothing further to watch out for, just crag and sun and tide.

All the world that swarmed with gods stripped down to their absence.

This is it,

the place that is everything in itself. Finally brought to this. Rough black rock at the edge of waves. The body alone, surrounded by the bare hardness of sea and sky and ground. The sound of breath there, the sound of every word cutting into the air. Space to be. To be space.

14.

I have just seen you go down the mountain:
I close the wicker gate in the setting sun.
The grass will be green again in the coming spring,
But will the wanderer ever return?

IT IS A rectangle consisting of four lines.

A picture.

Four lines not connected to anything else. Marked off by white space.

A picture that can almost be stepped into. That after looking at it long enough has been fully entered.

Green slope. Expanse of grass spreading in waves. On the far side of a fence.

Taken in at a glance it fills everything. Everything within the boundaries of the frame consists somehow of one substance. The memory of the wide screen of a cowboy movie. In the huge emptiness a tiny figure is moving downward. Black dot goes through a pass and vanishes. Grassy slope, with other grassy slopes beyond rolling out endlessly. Under white sky. The music of being swallowed up into distance.

Wanderer who does not return.

Where go the boats.

Already gone—**I have just seen you go down**—unbearable disappearance. The **mountain** will be there, **grass** will be there, absence will be there for all of time.

Eternity of returning seasons, eternity of the landscape of cowboy movies. A China which is eternal space. Ancient and abiding in this moment. Too vast to allow any certainty of returning to the point from which you set out.

Never to be summoned back but in these words. Who is the **wanderer**, who is it who may not return. The one you are least able to say goodbye to. Whose absence will put **mountain** and **sun** and **gate** and **grass** and **green** in question.

Will they be enough to make up the difference.

It has not happened yet. This is a prophecy of disappearance, in the form of a question. Is it even worse not to know.

All feeling bound up in the black dot already gone beyond sight. The green slopes go dark. Green to switch to black. Hills themselves to be yanked away as if tied to what went.

The words live in the sun that has not yet gone down. They are suspended in a place just emptied but where a presence is still felt. The words arranged in four lines are motionless and absolute. Nothing can move them out of place. The picture is complete and no part can be taken away. It can be gazed at as a way of inhabiting the completeness. Needs to be gazed at.

The final question also is always there.

will the wanderer ever return?

It is like being torn open just at the place where the picture reaches its limit.

15.

For in and out, above, about, below,
'Tis nothing but a Magic Shadow-show,
Play'd in a Box whose Candle is the Sun,
Round which we Phantom Figures come and go.

Awake! for Morning in the Bowl of Night
Has flung the Stone that puts the Stars to flight

—a book opened one morning from its first word issues a command—
Awake!—to consider the basic elements of

Morning and
Night and
Stars

at an age and in an age when to look at the night sky together with a like-minded friend was a great excitement—slipping in secret to the darkened lawn—out late enough to survey the pattern of stars from a suburban backyard—having by day looked at globes and telescopes and celestial atlases—paintings of molten or arid planetary surfaces—envisioning the system of orbits and gravitational pulls as a wider home, a future destination.

Omar Khayyám was supposed to have been an astronomer—in ancient Persia! watching stars from some rooftop in Isfahan!—and these quatrains were his music.

In each stanza each word moved like a satellite in obedience to an unvarying rhythm. There was constant astonishment at how the parts moved in relation to each other, balancing and responding and never getting in each other's way. A mechanical marvel. The weightless gears turn and each line advances into the next in an unbreakable continuing process like the planets in their orbits.

If you looked at the sky long enough you would understand everything. A writing was scattered across the night like the Persian script with which the book was ornamented.

To speak the lines was to summon into life names and wonders foreign and intricately textured—**Jamshýd's Sev'n-ring'd Cup**—**divine high piping Péhlevi**—**Kaikobád and Kaikhosrú**—**batter'd Caravanserai**—laid into patterns alongside **Wine** and **Rose** and **Garden** and **Bird** and **Treasure** and **River**.

Mosaic tiles intricately nested. Glittering Persian colors of cloud and ruby and gold. Mixed in with earthly tones of grass and pond water and garden soil. All the colors in the ultimate box of crayons.

The voice is old. It is wisdom music. The voice is springtime, watery freshness, new blossoms. It is like music for dancing. No desire for it ever to stop, as each line hooks into the next, a wheel forever turning—

> **And look—a thousand Blossoms with the Day**
> **Woke—and a thousand scatter'd into Clay**

—and only in the most gentle almost secret way murmurs that everything will in time be gone—all vanished, buried—**Dust into Dust, and under Dust, to lie—The Flower that once has blown forever dies**—a heartening sound.

The movement of the lines like the movement of a small boat through placid channels among reeds, for the pleasure of dipping the oar in once more and feeling the forward propulsion and the air of the lake, not afraid of any question—

> **Into this Universe, and *why* not knowing,**
> **Nor whence, like Water willy-nilly flowing**

—only delight in the solid weight of the push, the splendor of the colors at every turn, brisk and clipped and invigorating, a welcoming invitation.

And all the while the familiar locations give way as by the action of a folding screen to a different kind of space—

> **There was a Door to which I found no Key**

—a point where the invisible can be glimpsed—starry hidden molecular swirls, likewise moving in dance form, in a cadence accented with lutes or tambourines like those of ancient Persian musicians—

> **For in and out, above, about, below**

—the whirling of dervishes. The bearded prophets studying the night sky to find the most intimate secrets of

> **a magic Shadow-show**

and hide the secret in the syllables. Where they reside and move in and out of each other, trading places, even becoming each other, even while they lie motionless on the page, deathless graven carvings.

16.

I was of three minds,
Like a tree
In which there are three blackbirds.

—

A man and a woman
Are one.
A man and a woman and a blackbird
Are one.

—

It was evening all afternoon.
It was snowing
And it was going to snow.

HERE THE LINES are too short not to read. The words too isolated to hide anywhere.

The eye lands on

> **snowy mountains** and
> **tree** and
> **winds**.

They stand out on the page like a glittery Christmas card displayed on the mantel. The language of cold coming on. Pines covered in snow.

I was of three minds

Impossible to understand. Impossible not to understand. Who is "I"? Who was it who was like a tree with birds in it? Birds talking to each other inside the tree like three separate minds. Minds not agreeing with each other or not seeing the same things. In different parts of the tree.

Something being pried apart from within.

Being pulled different ways at the same time. Wanting to stay one and not able.

No, it cannot be. **A man and a woman and a blackbird** are three.

Like the first-grade primer that might say: This is a man. This is a woman. This is a blackbird.

It says so and doesn't. What is is the opposite of itself, it says.

The words **inflections** and **innuendoes** seen for the first time, understood and not understood. Understood only by the gap between **The blackbird whistling** and **just after**. It happens and after it happens there is nothing hanging in the air—**innuendoes**—a walloping silence.

The eye keeps coming back to what cannot be looked away from—

Icicles

The shadow of the blackbird

—and slides for the time being over **thin men of Haddam** and **noble accents** and **bawds of euphony**—unknown and bodiless phrases leaving no mark for now—moving on to where

**It marked the edge
Of one of many circles**

in a space made strange by snowfall—and to where

The river is moving

until everything is mixed together, its parts falling into itself.

It was evening all afternoon

and will stay that way forever

**It was snowing
And it was going to snow**

and there is nothing to say about it and nothing to think about it. It was and is going to be. It was night while it was still day. Already done and not yet begun. The snow would keep coming or else the snow that had not started had already been going on. And there was no way to tell, any more than to tell how three were one or one was three.

Except for these. The only signs found. Not having anything around them to get in their way.

Impossible to look away from the empty space around the words.

Open to that page when you want snow to be falling. For the comfort of a strangeness that does not go away.

In gold lettering on the spine the book is called MODERN. It is part of The Modern Library.

It is an old book with a particularly soft cloth binding.

17.

We thought the morning young, and lo! the moon
Again is bright.
Spring scarce has opened her fresh flowers,
When leaves are crimson-dyed.
Summer is with us yet:
Nay, the snow falls.
I watched the seasons pass:
Spring, summer, autumn, winter; a thousand trees,
A thousand flowers were strange and lovely in their
       pride.
So the time sped, and now
Fifty years of glory have passed by me,
And because they were a dream,
All, all has vanished and I wake
On the pillow where I laid my head,
The Pillow of Kantan.

HE DROVE JEEPS in Patton's army as far as the Elbe. Most of the hometown friends who signed up with him didn't get that far. Later he had trouble sleeping. He never talked about the war years.

After the surrender they sent him to Japan. They found a specialty for him—refrigeration—that would keep him on the army payroll for life. He met a young woman he wanted to marry but neither the army nor her family were keen on the idea. It took years—by then the Korean War had started—before the two were able to come to America together.

She spoke little English at first, and he less Japanese. In her low voice she began to tell her American nephew stories received at first as fragments only partly grasped—doll festivals—shoes being taken off before entering a house—parties under cherry trees in springtime. There were prints on the wall, brought back from Japan: people on a balcony watching snow fall, the full moon over a field of reeds swept by wind.

Some years later came the discovery in the city of a shop where Japanese objects were sold—sandals—cotton robes—toy bamboo flutes— writing brushes—a replica of a mask of a horned demon—a book with a photograph of the mask on which the replica was modeled.

On the first page of the book was a photograph of an empty stage.

Bare smooth wood. "A Nō stage is made entirely of cypress wood and is polished only with the natural oil of the wood."

It has its own arched rooftop upheld by pillars. A pine tree is painted on the back wall. To the left a colonnaded passageway leads away from the main playing area.

All of this within a larger auditorium, with rows of empty seats facing the empty stage.

There were said to be five types of plays: god plays, warrior plays, woman plays, madman plays, devil plays. But the book added: "The description is not altogether exact." Hundreds of plays, most never translated. Performed the same way since the fourteenth century.

Everything was almost impossible to describe or translate. The playwright Zeami referred to "disappearing and coming forth" passages. He said that "the moments of 'no action' are the most enjoyable." When the ghost or madman began to dance, the chorus spoke for him in chanted words. "The chanting is accompanied by the music of a flute, two hand-drums and sometimes a stick-drum." Available only for imagining, in the absence of a performance. A mask is worn by the principal actor. Unseen dance, unheard music, translation that could only ever be approximate. The replica of the demon mask hung on the wall and gazed at as if it might finally speak.

A theater held steady in the mind silent and invisible. Ghost theater where what was lost reappears and vanishes again. Longing persists after death. The dead return to the same place where they suffered or were abandoned. Ritual of all-night chanting, then silence.

Unseen dance where time stands still. A body moving in barely perceptible steps on an empty stage to the music of an inaudible flute.

Everything happening in the heart of nothing happening.

The young man dozes off on a pillow at a roadside inn and dreams he has been made emperor. Fifty years go by until he wakes suddenly, having slept for the length of time it took a bowl of millet to cook.

> **Whither are they gone that were so many...**
> **What I thought their voices**
> **Were but the whisperings of wind in the trees.**

Everything exact and brief—**the space of a dream**—waking in a deep gulp of air. Shiver of the sudden chill.

In this book and others the word "evanescent" kept recurring.

And the sound of wind in pines, of water trickling on rock—

> **The dew of flowers dripping day by day**
> **In how many thousand thousand years**
> **Will it have grown into a pool?**

—of bamboo flute on rocky shore, of torrent in mountain pass—a landscape made of flat pictures in books from which all clutter has been cleared. A space fullest where emptiest, with nothing to get in the way. Staring at the lines that describe it, it seems that the shapes of the letters themselves are part of it as they burn against the whiteness of the page surrounding them, ellipses and semi-colons and exclamation marks also are very much part of it.

> **Many times shall you behold**
> **The pale moon of dawn...**

Certain pages and certain phrases on those pages must be returned to—an uncountable number of times—as if to make sure they are still there. Not knowing what they give or what they preserve. Feeling but not knowing. To see a phrase. To speak it. To type it on a sheet of white paper.

Can this be called going beyond. Can this be called standing at the edge of going beyond.

18.

The flowers withered,
Their color faded away,
While meaninglessly
I spent my days in the world
And the long rains were falling.

AT THE LIBRARY, tucked away in a largely unvisited corner on the second floor, is a shelf of books about Japan and translations from Japanese and listings of translations from Japanese: plays, poems, novels, diaries, sketches and stories, Buddhist sutras, chronicles of clan warfare. By reading them it is possible to build up in mind a habitable place, sealed off in both time and space at least until the moment when Americans sailed into Edo Bay in 1853.

Within that world echoes went back and forth over centuries. Poems were changed into other poems. Poets became characters in plays. People in stories read poems written by people in other stories. What was repeated became different merely by changing a syllable or by being repeated at a different time in a different situation. A web of messages in the form of whispered hints.

Ono no Komachi was the mad beggarwoman astonishing the wandering priests in the Nō play *Sotoba Komachi*—

> **Oh piteous, piteous! Is this**
> **Komachi that once**
> **Was a bright flower,**
> **Komachi the beautiful**

—haunted by the ghost of a cruelly rejected lover—**My eyes dazzle. Oh the pain, the pain!**—rejected from her long-ago pride in the beauty that now has withered.

And here in another book was her poem from hundreds of years earlier, as if the connecting line had never been broken. As if it all came from a living source kept alive by being remembered and repeated.

Poem about disappearance, fading, uselessness, waste, monotony. Noise of uninterrupted rain. Life gone to ruin in isolation.

Brightness of **colors** seeming to gleam through rain in their absence. Painful feeling diffused through drenched air. A memory of lakeside downpour linking to that other solitary mind—Komachi gone some thousand years and continuing to exist in a dark perpetual rumble of melancholy—making contact as if with **rain**—the word itself imbued with essence of freshness—not faded or useless but wet, reviving, lively with the reflection of surrounding colors.

On another day in another book—a high school textbook printed in the 1920s—in the eighteenth-century graveyard elegy of Thomas Gray—

Full many a flower is born to blush unseen
And waste its sweetness on the desert air

—another burst of color is transmitted to empty space.

Centuries of signals arriving at unintended bays. Transitory arcs.

Where go the boats.

While the poet Komachi remains pent up in a habitation closed off by steady pelting rain, never going out. Unseen. Still there and full of regret.

19.

Away from the city that hurts and mocks
I'm standing alone by the desolate docks
In the still and the chill of the night

—

I cover the waterfront
In search of my love
And I'm covered by
A starless sky above

SURFACE NOISE AS the thick stylus hits the edge of the 78. Like surf sloshing against a pier.

Painting of a harbor at night. Painting of a woman singing. They come from the past. The record comes from the past.

She is here now. Ghost of yesterday as if coming through radio static. Billie Holiday.

No voice ever so clear. None so sharpened for its work of prying open. Turning each word inside out. Finding every recess of a syllable, tilting it around to find its joins and arcs and undersides. Does it mean the way it sounds or does it sound like what it means.

Each word is separated out—hefted into view, the veins of the sound positively made visible—shown from all sides, placed where it can be judged.

To hear the double **ll** in **still** and **chill** is to hear time stop, time being drilled into. Brought to a standstill and shuddering with cold.

Painting of the harbor at night. Edge of the unknown city. Geography of **desolate docks**—uninhabited wharves under **starless sky**.

A vowel need not be prolonged to sound an immeasurable depth or distance. The precision of the instrument measures an arc by which the full extent can be gauged.

An abandoned place, part of a map of incompleteness—no one is around—

Oh how I yearn

—bare edge—edge of pier, edge of consonant—as her voice is edge sounding both. Night sky made of sound.

A voice in the cold dark, its sound the only warmth, penetrating all the space around it.

Every word spoken as much as any word could ever be spoken.

Fully uttered, an alarm traveling over water.

20.

starry dynamo in the machinery of night

supernatural darkness of cold-water flats

blind streets of shuddering cloud

backyard green tree cemetery dawns

drear light of Zoo

THE OLDER BROTHER who at ten recited Kipling

and at thirteen read aloud (at the dinner table for maximum effect) the shocking final paragraphs of Mickey Spillane novels

and at fourteen favorite paragraphs from J. D. Salinger

and at fifteen the liner notes of Riverside and Prestige albums and interviews from *Down Beat* and *Metronome*

and at sixteen the opening lines of "The Love Song of J. Alfred Prufrock"

at seventeen returned on the late train from Penn Station with books of new words or words newly found, *The Subterraneans* by Jack Kerouac and *A Devil in Paradise* by Henry Miller and *A Season in Hell* by Arthur Rimbaud and *A Spy in the House of Love* by Anaïs Nin and *Memoirs of a Shy Pornographer* by Kenneth Patchen and *The Palm-Wine Drinkard* by Amos Tutuloa and *Cain's Book* by Alexander Trocchi and *A Hundred Camels in the Courtyard* by Paul Bowles and *Gasoline* by Gregory Corso and *Jazz Its Evolution and Essence* by André Hodeir and *The Beats* and *The Angry Black* and *Hiparama of the Classics* by Lord Buckley and *Marijuana Girl* by N. R. DeMexico and *Howl and Other Poems* by Allen Ginsberg

all of which became an encyclopedia of new words and new facts, its pages inseparable from the lingering smell of his cigarettes,

a secret course of instruction where because everything was unknown everything was relevant, any stray recognizable landmark a possible guide in the labyrinth

the labyrinth being the unknown city at night, interiors of imagined apartments materialized out of smoke and visualized along lines provided by television shows about urban delinquents, barely furnished kitchens seen through a semi-transparent screen, the silhouettes of the bodies moving on the other side of it lit by candles after midnight, saxophone motif seeping in from a bar on the corner,

the stuff of alluring melodramatic movie posters,

now actually named and located—in **cold-water flats—blind streets— cemetery dawns—rooftops—hotels—traffic light—ashcan—Zoo— Bickford's—jukebox**—travelogue of unvisited early morning hours.

Pasted on the page as in a stamp album: **Peyote solidities of halls** were the solidities of the letters forming the words and the shapes they made in doing so, the components of **Peyote** assembling into an unknowable presence—what can it signify?—a word that is itself a wavering presence almost tasted, summoned from some closely lurking beyond—making **halls** strange—to find they had always been so.

21.

When I heard the learn'd astronomer,
When the proofs, the figures, were ranged in columns
      before me,
When I was shown the charts and diagrams, to add,
      divide, and measure them,
When I sitting heard the astronomer where he lectured
      with much applause in the lecture-room,
How soon unaccountable I became tired and sick,
Till rising and gliding out I wander'd off by myself,
In the mystical moist night-air, and from time to time,
Look'd up in perfect silence at the stars.

When I heard—
When the proofs—
When I was shown—
When I sitting heard the astronomer—

the rhythm of a Babylonian inscription. A history measured in repetitions. The compiling of a list like the inventory of a dynastic palace—**proofs—figures—columns—charts—diagrams—**each item the starting point for an even longer list, an index of indexes, until to comprehend it the line must get longer and longer—

When I sitting heard the astronomer where he lectured
with much applause in the lecture room—

long enough to run out of breath to the point of dizziness, in a crowded hall, airless and hot—oppressed by the need **to add, divide, and measure—** recoiling from the thud of **much applause—**until

How soon unaccountable I became tired and sick

—how unexpected for him to say it, to seize up in the middle of his own lines as if he cannot go on—drained by headache, faintness, dehydration, the nausea of tedium—

I became tired and sick

—startled that he should display fatigue, weakness—a malaise like that instilled by reading the lines themselves, not from the idea of astronomy but merely of charts, figures, adding and dividing—a wall of arithmetic— and with it the premonition of a numeric adulthood, the anticipation of tax forms, insurance forms, contracts, license applications, school applications, job applications, the blank sameness of documents spread across a kitchen table—a life sentence of quantitative assignments—under hot overhead lights—

Till rising and gliding out

having by slippery transformation attained the power of gliding

In the mystical-moist night-air

—and in that single unbroken step the whole body having passed from one condition to another—**wander'd** from arid light into moist darkness—to a solitary lawn outside the hall—the refreshment of night air—where **from time to time**—in the liberty of having no imposed schedule, no forced attendance—

Look'd up in perfect silence at the stars

—the body finds itself again fully open—at perfect ease—joined with darkness and reviving freshness of night air as if the body were not separate from them—a place to be found only by instinct, by **gliding**.

22.

Earth, Air, Water heaved and turned in darkness,
No living creatures knew that land, that sea
Where heat fell against cold, cold against heat—
Roughness at war with smooth and wet with drought,
Things that gave way entered unyielding masses,
Heaviness fell into things that had no weight.

THE WORDS ARE carved pieces. Slide them into rows. Each row links up with the next, row after row until it makes a book that can contain everything. An ancient device like an abacus or lyre. The parts click together in rhythm and generate pictures, tastes, odors, noises, voices, textures of every kind of surface, whether of crag or leaf or flesh.

Taken one at a time the pieces appear simple

reef   sand   heat   cold   smooth   wet

—tiles that might be picked out from a game set to be combined into unforeseeable patterns.

It is a creation of the world out of nothingness—

**lakes, springs, dancing waterfalls
streamed downhill into valleys, waters glancing
through rocks, grass and wild-flowered meadows**

—out of words that are nothing until put next to other words where for a moment in combination they become a further different thing—and then, as the linking advances according to its rhythm, warp into something else again—a process never ending and continuously exciting—

**grapes
dropping from the vine, cherry, strawberry
ripened in silver shadows of the mountain**

—and ominous with emerging forms of destruction—

**all that drives men to avarice and murder
shone in the dark: the loot was dragged to light
and War, inspired by curse of iron and gold,
lifted blood-clotted hands and marched the earth—**

as leaf folds over leaf, vine entwines fresh shoots among the curlicues of an iron gate, and life erupts and mutates along paths that lead nowhere except toward the next transition into an altered form.

When they have aroused even the slightest anger from a god, these spirit bodies of the most ancient inhabitants are changed into rivers, trees, birds. The birds themselves change from white to black. The changes become stories told as a prelude to other changes—there is barely time to say anything before transformation stops up the voice—

her gift of speech was ripped away and from her throat came guttural noises horrible to hear

—horror upon horror, washed along in the same cadence as rivers and the blossoming meadows along their banks. Sinuous and delightful forms in sunlight are translated into scenes of vengeance that in turn melt back into configurations of stars and flowers. Vistas of meadow and sky still pulse with the violence they were made from.

An unfolding irresistible current. Carried as on a raft through gulfs and floating mists. All made of words that are so clear on the page they seem placed there to show themselves as words and nothing more. Light, airy, with sun suffusing them—**lonely in a field a white ox wanders—wet hair branched in antlers—tears stirred the pool to waves—in flickering drops of blood among their feathers—I've driven rivers back to springs and fountains**—a living dictionary woven out of terrors and desires. Words tremble at sensing other words in close proximity.

23.

Claude Allen and his dear old father
Have met their fatal doom at last
Their friends are glad their trouble's ended
And hope their souls are now at rest

Poor Claude was young and very handsome
And still had hopes until the end
That he might in some way or other
Escape his death at Richmond's pen

But the governor being so hard-hearted
Not caring what his friends might say
He finally took his sweet life from him
In the cold ground his body lay

Claude's mother's tears were gently flowing
All for the one she held so dear
It seemed no one could tell her trouble
It seemed no one could tell but her

Poor Claude he had a pretty sweetheart
She mourns the loss of the one she loved
She hopes to meet beyond the river
A fair young face in Heaven above

High up on yonder's lonely mountain
Claude Allen lays beneath the clay
No more we hear his words of mercy
Or see his face till the Judgment Day

Now all young men from this take warning
Be careful how you go astray
Or you might end like poor Claude Allen
And have this awful debt to pay

CLAUDE ALLEN AND his father Floyd were electrocuted on March 28, 1913. They had been convicted of murder following a gun battle the previous year in a courtroom in Carroll County, Virginia, in which the judge, the prosecutor, the sheriff, and two others were killed. Floyd had been sentenced, moments earlier, to a year in prison for a minor felony. It was not determined who fired the first shot.

The musician Clarence Ashley was eighteen years old at the time of the execution. He recorded the ballad of it almost fifty years later.

A ballad was the sound not of what happened once only on a particular day but of what would always happen. The dead would continue to be encountered **beyond the river**. A governor would not care **what his friends might say**. Outlaws would speak **words of mercy**. **Judgment Day** and **fatal doom** are fixed. Sorrow is unknowable to any but the one who sorrows:

> **It seems no one could tell her trouble**
> **It seems no one could tell but her**

It is another language making use of the same words as the everyday one. The more simple the words the more completely they say what cannot even be translated. Like a headstone.

Everything is written down forever even if in the course of years some of the words change and the song splits into different versions. The deed is inscribed. If

> **He finally took his sweet life from him**

there is no scraping it out. Tears **gently flowing** remain so, unsupportable pain frozen outside of time.

Everything has already happened in this America somehow more real than shopping center or television special or Dodge showroom. **Yonder's lonely mountain**. A durable figure chipped out of rock wall. **Young and very handsome**. Portrait from which the features have darkened past recognition. It could be anybody. **From this take warning**. It already happened and it will happen again.

Sound of an old doom. Sorrows and rages unrecoverable except through the gaps in the hand-hewn monument, almost every part of it smoothed away by now but for the weathered framework.

Bare shape accented by damages, as an old man's voice is damaged by time.

24.

There is no whiskey in this town
There is no bar to sit us down

Where is the telephone
Is here no telephone

Oh sir goddamn me no

FOR SOME REASON—professional needs or random curiosity or the yearning to acquire mysterious capabilities—or merely the thought that somebody in the family might find them useful—the house began to fill up with language records. A complete course of instruction in conversational French: **En faisant du ski je me suis cassé la jambe**. And then, following the same template, in German: **Ich habe mich beim Ski das Bein gebrochen**. Spanish and Italian were also made available.

Then came a series of small yellow-covered hardbound books purchased at a steep discount: *Teach Yourself Greek. Teach Yourself Russian. Teach Yourself Finnish. Teach Yourself Samoan.* Nothing was funnier than some of the sentences provided as translation exercises.

All the talk of languages led to the rediscovery of a slender volume tucked long ago into an odd corner of a bookcase. *Japanese in Thirty Hours* had been brought back from Tokyo sometime after the war. It was filled with odd statements:

> **I brought nineteen pencils.**
> **That I read this book was a good thing.**
> **I am the person who played tennis.**
> **What is the thing which is here?**

To say these aloud made the act of speaking unfamiliar. There were occasional hilarious experiments in trying to talk in the manner of foreign language primers.

In the opera *The Rise and Fall of the City of Mahagonny* by Bertolt Brecht and Kurt Weill, two songs in English were interpolated in the German libretto, the "Alabama Song" and the "Benares Song." On the recording the voice of Lotte Lenya came through singing in an English made into something other—

> **Where is the telephone**
> **Is here no telephone**

—being sung in the opera in an Alaska which was also not Alaska. Everything was made completely flat and completely strange. Bertolt Brecht was the proponent of something called the Alienation Effect. It sounded even better in German, and when repeated became a harsh sort of magic spell—*Verfremdungseffekt, Verfremdungseffekt*—from the verb *verfremden*: to make strange, or other, or another's. The peculiar English of those songs might be an example of that effect.

Take something ordinary—almost mindlessly so, any accidental fact—deformed just slightly, or separated from where it ought to be, and by that becoming truly peculiar, and making everything around it peculiar. Suddenly exposed it was no longer recognizable. It seemed you had gotten so used to surface arrangements—the place where a chair or a window or a road seen from a window was—as to forget what they were arrangements of. It was like not knowing where you had been living.

The voice of Lotte Lenya had that effect anyway. What she did was a kind of singing not entirely like what was usually called singing. Any words, even

To Benares Johnny let us go

seemed to have been dragged through a very rough landscape, and marked with dents and scrapes of sarcastic awareness ever after. It was a voice suited to recounting what otherwise would not be believed. She came from the other world of refugees and displaced persons which had just been Europe and was still here among us, in shadows, where there was more to hear if anyone wished to know. Europe of camps and death marches like a black-and-white after-impression hanging in the air of 1960. News coming twenty years late to children. That had already come late twenty years before. In a theater in Greenwich Village she sang "Pirate Jenny"—

Kill them now, or later?

Lotte Lenya, Bertolt Brecht, Kurt Weill. These were names not of motionless figures but of a series of actions in response to shifting unavoidable circumstances. History as continuous unsteady churn. Trapdoors the size of countries. Uprooted from one place to a different one and always speaking at least in part the language of the place fled from. So no language could ever have been pure. Only unstable mixtures at risk of fragmenting. Held together moment to moment by a work not imagined before, of untangling and substituting, clearing out buildups of debris, assembling auxiliary passageways and barricades from whatever materials came to hand. Compensating for whatever essential elements had drifted beyond retrieval.

An object acquired strange power from being moved from its position. The simplest sentence could be shifted out of its own meaning and undermine all sentences around it by a ripple effect. A shiver of the alien that could make anything absurd or frightful.

Look at any cluster of words long enough—catch hold of a phrase spoken thoughtlessly out of habit—and they became indistinguishable from what was sometimes called broken English.

Are they so fragile.

Breaking them in pieces makes them stand out more. Like a weather-damaged or partly ripped poster on the wall of a construction site.

The incisions and scratchmarks from which the city is patched together. Pasted one alongside another.

25.

Jungle Moon Men

ONLY THAT. THE name of a movie not seen. A tiny slug of type among the television listings for the early morning hours. With a dismissive critical comment, "Title tells it" or "Like it sounds." An adventure of Jungle Jim. Never seen.

The title—beating like a bongo—that made a pocket for itself in the mind.

Jungle Moon Men

Only that and nothing more. The occasion of a secret and irresistible laughter. Why is that so funny. Or why if it is funny does it prompt unexpected wonder or even unease. Here is where meaning failed.

It was as if you had gone looking for what could truly be called mindless and having found it wondered why. What was the delight of the empty. Or was it not. Could anything be empty that even uttered silently involved such decisive actions of tongue and palate and lips. A whole inner geography wrapped in a cluster of syllables. To be spoken in the cavernous narrational rumble of coming attractions for the Saturday matinee

Jungle Moon Men

—a title that existed because it had to. It was already its own movie, no actual movie could deliver that promised ecstasy of inanity, that marriage of jungle and moon, that fusing of dream elements into a new compound.

A dream not to be glimpsed past its cluttered anteroom, visible through the half-open portal. Whatever you might want to add to it already detracts from its undiluted solitariness. Therefore it would be wiser not to see the movie. Better to grope along the edges of what does not want to be defined or made visible. A talismanic gem that light cannot penetrate perceptible only by means of opaque syllables withholding anything like a story.

Jungle Moon Men

Astral messenger. A compressed meteorite fallen to the planet's surface beyond the reach even of Jungle Jim. Title as door jammed shut or indecipherable code. Its only known function to set off that wellspring of delirious laughter fusing with inexplicable awe.

The only thing to do perhaps is to appropriate it and thereby emulate the arcane worship of some lost or obliterated cult. Find words for which it might serve as title, a kind of prayer to the unknown. A fit of giggles slipping out like a plume of sacrificial incense.

26.

Fog everywhere. Fog up the river, where it flows among green aits and meadows; fog down the river, where it rolls defiled among the tiers of shipping, and the waterside pollutions of a great (and dirty) city. Fog on the Essex marshes, fog on the Kentish heights. Fog creeping into the cabooses of collier-brigs; fog lying out on the yard, and hovering in the rigging of great ships; fog drooping on the gunwales of barges and small boats. Fog in the eyes and throats of ancient Greenwich pensioners, wheezing by the firesides of their wards; fog in the stem and bowl of the afternoon pipe of the wrathful skipper, down in his close cabin; fog cruelly pinching the toes and fingers of his shivering little 'prentice boy on deck. Chance people on the bridges peeping over the parapets into a nether sky of fog, with fog all round them, as if they were up in a balloon, and hanging in the misty clouds.

THE PARAGRAPH PERMEATED by fog in *Bleak House* emerged as a broad cloudlike shape. From a distance, even before more than a few words became clear, a geography was visible like the view from a low-flying plane, a marsh or craggy bluff of words, with streams or interweaving roads connecting its parts, the whole of it seeming to breathe, glisten, give off its particular climatic aroma.

Paragraphs like that could go on for long unfolding stretches. To enter them was to participate in movement, measure proportions by eye, be part of an intricately operating subterritory. Each separate world with its own elements, the Costaguana of Conrad's *Nostromo* where

> **At night the body of clouds advancing higher up
> the sky smothers the whole quiet gulf below with an
> impenetrable darkness, in which the sound of the
> falling showers can be heard beginning and ceasing
> abruptly—now here, now there… The few stars left
> below the seaward frown of the vault shine feebly as
> into the mouth of a black cavern**

—or the Roman catacombs of Hawthorne's *Marble Faun*, divisible into broken pieces of language fitted together with bits of indistinguishable paste—

> **vast tomb—a sort of dream—reminiscences of church-
> aisles and grimy cellars—broken into fragments and
> hopelessly intermingled—a dark-red, crumbly stone—
> the shape of a human body was discernible in white
> ashes—through a crevice a little daylight glimmered
> down—peeped into a burial niche—by abrupt rudely
> hewn steps into deeper and deeper recesses of the
> earth—narrow and tortuous passages—**

or Melville's Pacific capable of holding anything—

> **It rolls the midmost waters of the world, the Indian
> ocean and Atlantic being but its arms. The same waves
> wash the moles of the new-built Californian towns,
> but yesterday planted by the recentest race of men, and**

lave the faded but still gorgeous skirts of Asiatic lands, older than Abraham; while all between float milky-ways of coral isles, and low-lying, endless, unknown Archipelagoes, and impenetrable Japans. Thus this mysterious, divine Pacific zones the world's whole bulk about; makes coasts one bay to it; seems the tide-beating heart of earth—

or Faulkner's aviator in *Pylon* intruding into the unwelcoming space of a high-class clothing emporium—

his rubber soles falling in quick hissing thuds on pavement and iron sill and then upon the tile floor of that museum of hats and ties and shirts, the beltbuckles and cufflinks and handkerchiefs, the pipes shaped like golfclubs and the drinking tools shaped like boots and barnyard fowls and the minute impedimenta for wear on ties and vestchains shaped like bits and spurs, resembled biologic specimens put into the inviolate preservative before they had ever been breathed into—

a different sea-change every time, every word transmuted into an inhabitant of that distinct place, eroded by that air and marked by that soil, made habitable for different creatures. Made of different things even if the words may be the same. They exist together and bring about changes in what neighbors them. They extend inward, make progressions through portals only made apparent by continuing to crawl forward into what seems not to end.

These are not even stories. These are the wetlands where stories grow. Vegetation, or coastal rock forms, or half-finished housing developments.

The page wriggles. From above it is a sort of jungle or luminous murk. The paragraph can be spotted moving even with the eyes only half focused, the separate words not made out at all except as familiar but only blurrily recognized shapes heaving and coalescing into some new organism—a more total sense comes through the pattern of slithers in which the words move together like a body.

These patches have points of beginning and points of ending but in between are tracts of endlessness. Once inside you might be there forever. Reading becomes something like the idea of writing. A continuous act never done.

27.

I can't

speak—my tongue is broken;
a thin flame runs under
my skin; seeing nothing,

hearing only my own ears
drumming, I drip with sweat;
trembling shakes my body

and I turn paler than
dry grass

WRITING FROM INSIDE so that words themselves are of the body. The private and barely detected made audible—

**a thin flame runs under
my skin**

—and remaining so in a fragment surviving accidental or deliberate destruction. Secret desire running like an underground river through dark Christian centuries. Not a symbol but the body itself trembling and sweating in the immediacy of what might as well be now—or is now.

Body in Aegean light. Flesh made not of dead stone but quivering speech even if

my tongue is broken

—don't go looking anywhere for a comparison, the measure is at hand in the tongue-tied trembling reader. A unison of incompleteness, of being broken off. Eternity of the momentary.

Sappho. The thought of a scroll of her complete poems rolled up somewhere. Somewhere in the heaven of lost books.

To think of the violent motion in the midst of which everything happened—cities thrown in fires—unrecorded burial pits—erased names—

trembling shakes my body

—one body near another, feeling what is unspoken, occupying all space and thought. What is small and hidden—silent—more immense than anything.

Interior immensity. Shard.

A living body. Was there. Is there.

28.

A savage place! as holy and enchanted
As e'er beneath a waning moon was haunted
By woman wailing for her demon-lover!

–

A damsel with a dulcimer
In a vision once I saw:

–

Ancestral voices prophesying war!

–

Weave a circle round him thrice,
And close your eyes with holy dread,
For he on honey-dew hath fed,
And drunk the milk of Paradise.

"IF A MAN could pass through Paradise in a dream, and have a flower presented to him as a pledge that his soul had really been there, and if he found that flower in his hand when he awoke—Ay! and what then?" This passage from a notebook of Samuel Taylor Coleridge, quoted in the magazine *Film Culture* in 1963, was received as a challenge. There were questions acknowledged to be unanswerable. Here was one that announced itself as unaskable.

Unless "Kubla Khan" was itself that flower as much as anything could be. The impossible proof, like the flower that Rod Taylor brought back from the future—the flower Yvette Mimieux gave him—in the movie of *The Time Machine.*

The object that by its existence smashes the separation between incommensurable worlds.

The poem is a record of broken passage, partial transmission. A pure voice blocked and fragmented. Only the pure part left standing, the rest or most of the rest fallen back into the unknowable. The remnant having forced its way through sits there incomplete and beyond explanation. It resists having its blanks filled in or being made into a story. Protects itself against exposure to daylight. Protects itself against being understood.

To the extent that what is found in the hand on waking is incomprehensible—that the links have dissolved leaving only emblems of mysteries—proof has been given. Whatever is clearly graspable must be false.

Ay! and what then?

There is no imaginable completed version of "Kubla Khan"—to have woken from a dream is to know that. Whatever cannot get through stays on the other side beyond retrieval. Unless the dreamt prove true or the unaskable question turn out to be its own answer. Unless the visible world is dismantled to reveal another.

The **woman wailing** and the **ancestral voices** and the **symphony and song** of the **maiden with a dulcimer** must break off before they are properly heard—a wavelength deflected, warped beyond reception—like the chasm slanted athwart—everything oblique and turned in a reverse direction—and breaking apart in its center to reveal what is least expected or understood, a prophecy of **war**. A hole opens up—the connection is torn, that vast world suddenly lost. The poem we have is perhaps not even the poem, but merely some sort of buffer poem formed to heal the gap.

As if an all-obliterating **war** raged in remotest depths. A place like the center of the sun. Not to be looked at or inhabited.

Every part of the poem disappears and is replaced by another. A process of continual replacement never completed. Nothing but tokens of what is lost. Words representing other words. Tokens replaced by further tokens,

ceaseless turmoil seething

leaving as debris a series of occult signs.

Here is the point of entry into that famous mystery The Occult. The name for what is most desired. Desired because not to be contacted by any ordinary means. Not to be revealed except sideways—only to be haunted by—or seen with other eyes, latent alternate eyes obscurely sensed to exist—but in what body?—sensed through the medium of unseeing words. Words see what eyes cannot.

Within the **circle** woven around **thrice**—in the words of the charm—is the very **milk of Paradise**—here—to be drunk by being uttered.

The true charm. Gate entered by no way but saying.

Remnant of **holy dread** hovering in air.

Laudanum, the kids talked about after class. The milk of paradise was laudanum.

"Kubla Khan" was a shared dream anthem. An occasion for silent nods and secret glances. We are here eternally together.

Archaic radio. Transmitted from a ruined cottage in the ancient lake country.

29.

Rose-cheek'd Laura, come,
Sing thou smoothly with thy beauty's
Silent music, either other
Sweetly gracing.

Lovely forms do flow
From concent divinely fraḿed;
Heav'n is music, and thy beauty's
Birth is heavenly.

These dull notes we sing
Discords need for helps to grace them;
Only beauty purely loving
Knows no discord,

But still moves delight,
Like clear springs renew'd by flowing,
Ever perfect, ever in them-
Selves eternal.

WHERE IS THE poem. In what manner of space does it exist.

In air. Self-levitated. A glistening mobile.

The facets of it giving off light as it turns.

Body everywhere transparent.

All its turnings one movement.

In an air. It is music made of words. Light made of music. The unknown made of light.

And strong enough to be kicked like the fender of a car. Ethereal metal.

It makes its sounds with the senses of living bodies. Tunes their brains into inward amplifier. Unsounded sound the acutest possible vibration.

Every part of it has a weight balancing every other part, **either other sweetly gracing**, every part of it is part of the one action it is, it demonstrates what it is in being there in the air, it is not about anything but its own harmony, it already is where it is going, it

still moves delight

still and always

ever perfect

through all the stages of an orbital dance,

thy beauty's birth

in ancient courtly measure made aerial, the salutes and bows described by syllabic tunings, alive with the movement of a current

like clear streams renew'd by flowing

whose flow is within this, circulates within its parts. And it does not ever end but flows back within itself, finding its endless wholeness.

Existing apart. In its **Heaven**. Bound to the life around it only by a name—

Laura

—she the player of the **silent music** of which all this wants to be the

approximation. A plea for a perfection of **concent**. Which is music
consenting to be concert.

It lives on in the dark as a kind of disembodied flute phrase

like clear streams renew'd by flowing

with other Elizabethan sounds coming back in chorale, joined by the
falsetto radio ballads of Smokey Robinson or Curtis Mayfield,

        weep you no more sad fountains

or

        the silver swan who living had no note

or

        I saw my lady weep

or

        I must go walk the wood so wild

or

        are those clear fires that vanish into smoke

or

        thrice toss these oaken ashes in the air

or

        follow thy fair sun unhappy shadow

or

        like melting snow upon some craggy hill

they move through the darkness in sweet concert. Stream of forms.

30.

Licence my roaving hands, and let them go,
Before, behind, between, above, below.
O my America! my new-found land

—and in the midst of everything else to be overtaken by sex and to be overtaken by history in the same moment, struck by the incalculable weight of what was falling down, a burden of excitement, an eagerness in perking up to a new sense of ancient dangers once again transmitted—

language being a body and a body a part of history—involved in transmission, in being transmitted—consonants are substance, vowels breath—grammar flexes and circulates energies—utterance is the borderland, history is the story of borderlands.

The body wakes to language as to love, to the translating of shadow into substance—

> **where shadows do for bodies stand**
> **thou may'st be abused if thy sight be dim**

—and substance into shadow—

> **are they shadows that we see**
> **and can shadows pleasures give**

—so that an intermingling

> **makes both one, each this and that—**

where all that is is verb, whether moving as in Donne's elegy

> **before, behind, between, above, below**

in a paradise of fulfilled desire, of substance come into its own, taking as its own the language of privateers and colonial explorers, sea-rovers licensed by monarchical seal, or

> **in and out, above, about, below**

in Fitzgerald's magic shadow-show where all are phantoms in a child's toy theater.

To find yourself where the center is and has always been, in the midst of unbroken continuity, totality of all regions and eras within reach—

all here in one bed lay

as a worldwide network of signals converges on a body no longer imaginary. The sun no longer imaginary. Body through which all else becomes real, by currents running through a system of nerves—all dreads and delights promiscuously authentic and at hand

—until it becomes urgent to find the means to scrape away the concealing accumulated strata of households, ocean crossings, cities, marriages, contracts, incursions, enforced registries, secret concealed memoranda, linked in a living map where all points connect back and forth. Traces of every voyage and freebooting inroad find their way into words. Cordage. Clumps of crushed trinkets or burned dwellings settle around them. Basement storehouses cracked open. Mill wheels of the real perceptible as splinters and gutters.

To salvage light from mold and trash-heaps, the slang and slurs of guards and smugglers, clutter full of discarded intentions. Distractions of time and accident. Footnotes in place of breathable air. To find or force a way to what is uncorrupted and still moist. (Footnote: still = always.) The radiant center, only existent when revived now, spoken aloud. To find among inventions, ribbons, umber shadows, floods of satin folds, the trembling of the permanently alive.

To insist on believing in one interconnected organism, expanse of uninterrupted speech, penetrating time along the lines of a network somehow secret. To stare until you hear the innermost tone the rest of the paraphernalia is hung on.

Words measured by living bodies. Or bodies mapped by meter.

Let sea-discoverers to new worlds have gone
Let maps to other, worlds on worlds have shown

From earth to air and air to earth. Verb into flesh and back again.
The sexual body wants a language and takes what it can recognize.
The words are shaped with the weight of the atmosphere they feed on. Spoken aloud in a room the room bends its form to them.
The solid is all a vibration.
We come to inhabit substantial glimmer.
The poem is mere rim, the skin of what otherwise is not to be seen at all. Without it we would be invisible.

31.

A dog starvd at his Masters Gate
Predicts the ruin of the State

–

Each outcry of the hunted Hare
A fibre from the Brain does tear

–

Every Morn & every Night
Some are Born to sweet delight
Some are Born to sweet delight
Some are Born to Endless Night

Blake came barging into everything, a fracture having nothing to do with books already studied, or correct answers to anything, speaking from what was now the past but having already at its point of coming into being refused ever to be the past, continuing to operate from a place deeper than hip moderns in shades who could blend at last into movie poster for the Golden Gate Bridge or flute music for a Sunday afternoon,

his accepted brethren whom, tyrant, he calls free

while

the just man rages in the wilds
Where lions roam

—wilds that were cities, now polluted wreckage whose pieces cannot again fit pleasurably together as in a magazine supplement—unless everything were made over, or else not to have lived at all—

Sooner murder an infant in its cradle than nurse unacted desires

—oppressed in the shadow of what others had already built—in the state whose ruin prophesied by token of the starved dog is already under way—bleeding walls and gasoline and smoke seep from between widescreen billboards for car movies and newly invented skin creams.

The brain—yours or someone else's—has fibers—torn from it by the torture of an animal. The mirrors will have splintered, and history flattened to a wall chart in the deserted classroom, of the timeline leading from the Roman empire to the advent of mercantilism.

Somewhere here was the center of a life but whose. Where is **the mental traveler** going. Who is **the mental traveler**. Blake a medium lending voice to a past that continues to know more than a future he has already sensed. The words shiver and slip out of themselves, reverse to show their true side. Incomprehensible and thus true prophecy.

A hidden door, present and at hand, perpetually about to be opened.

He came to function as a code for messages not necessarily decryptable even by those who sent them.

Not to be explained. To be scraped by it and haunted—**Every Morn & every Night**—hanging in the midst where mills grind. Fires, manacles, invisible worms, groans, dismay, the enmity of spiders.

Type out these lines to see if the meanings can be changed or found. A magical act. So that if your friend is lost or suffering you are to establish communication by the transfer of this piece of paper.

Might you read it together, as chart for an escape like that of outlaws headed for outer territories. Desert land without mist or foggy woods, devoid of coastal vistas, only the arid canyon where

Body is a portion of the Soul discernd by the five Senses

—inhabiting **Contraries**—goaded out of restfulness.

To think to save her—counterpart on the edge of some irrevocable descent—with Blake, as if this scroll were antitoxin or ancient Egyptian healing incantation. Heal a sick love. Turn venoms into their **contraries**. If not with Blake then what is his use. Or cry out for instruction even at this late hour—otherwise incapable and without resources—since

The authors are in Eternity

32.

I lean my elbows on the table, the lamp shines brightly on these newspapers I am fool enough to read again, these stupid books.

At an enormous distance above my subterranean parlor, houses take root, fogs gather. The mud is red or black. Monstrous city, night without end!

HERE YOU ARE sidelined. You have come to where you have never mattered.

Here a wall

this whitewashed tomb

is mirror giving back blank chill. A necessary exhaustion before it is possible even to begin.

To begin is to discard. To have come to the barrier without advancing a single step. To have sat immobilized as if an action were being performed—nothing more than recognition of helplessness. An act of waiting out what cannot bestow anything and can only confirm an emptying that already occurred. No signal to be given beyond a single word: Departure.

To have been always at the same desk among newspapers and books, arbitrary historical quotations or statistical charts muttered aloud out of a habit drained even of motive, television listings, railroad schedules, souvenirs of motels and famous ice cream parlors.

Carried along by drift, the involuntary passenger in a salon in a Jules Verne submarine many miles below the polar cap. At the far end of the interior—lit by the unreal glow of gas lamps—the captain is sighted, his back turned, not allowing himself to be gazed at, perhaps turned to stone, permanently immobilized.

I am master of silence

Here the will to escape finds a final domed enclosure. Corridors of limestone, abandoned hydraulic systems. A space in which to be erased, inhabiting the myth of an unending vigil. You park yourself somewhere out of view, vestigial unclaimed luggage. The question becomes whether you have enough energy to be in the place where you happen to find yourself. Anything that once seemed easy was a board game of the simple kind that children like. The suitcase is full of them, their grids faded and the dice gone astray.

For lack of other amusement you listen to the voice of the worn-out child who has already peered into the end of everything. A prophet with no prophecy other than

the semblance of an opening

in the grip of an involuntary shiver. How to speak. With what. Having woken to find no one there where you thought you had been.

The chill breeze between the walls making a noise like a vacuum cleaner in an adjacent apartment.

Somebody else is me and is sitting in my chair reading a book he no longer understands.

"He was about done and you haven't started yet."

33.

Tearful city
      on a summer's day
the hard grey
      dwindling
in a wall of
      rain—

THE WOMAN WHO told me to read Gary Snyder also recommended William Carlos Williams. She was a poet and I figured she could tell me what I needed to make contact with to go beyond cherished pages in old books that had come to seem like a stamp collection or a manila folder guarding the souvenirs of childhood: a plan of Fort Ticonderoga, a napkin from a roadside Howard Johnson's. Private incommunicable associations of no further use. Everything of worth, capable of providing sustenance, was in the future—including the undiscovered past. So after spending time with *Riprap* and *Cold Mountain Poems* and *Myths & Texts* I ventured to purchase the New Directions hardcover *The Collected Earlier Poems of William Carlos Williams*—an expensive item at the time, all of $5—and carried it around for months simply reading from one end to the other— as easy as stepping into water—constantly drawn to it but not getting it, overwhelmed by the variousness of the signals. It was like stepping into a noisy street, again and again, woken but finding it hard to focus on any one face or window or discarded object, finally lost in a crowd of others, part of it, not seeing but seen, caught in the lens in the very moment of looking through it.

Where is this crowd? Had I dreamt of this? That there could be a poetry that was itself the world? That could be walked around in, inhaled?

It existed, that was all. Not as a demand but as a gift, the sudden lifting of a pervasive tension. A line traveled to the nerve-endings. In one go mind and body opened up as the page opened up, accordion-like. There was an uncanny feeling of stepping into a different kind of depth—uncanny because the page was so plainly flat, and Williams was doing his all to insist on the flatness. Ordinary words isolated in white space. There they were. The eye took them in in one gulp, like an unprepared view of road and bushes and vines. In the chaos of the visible the most solid chunks of matter turned phantasmal, and then switched back into the unnatural clarity of field or railroad embankment or segment of varnished floor.

A barrier dissolved—a fog that had been hanging around words—I could see what my thoughts were made of.

> **bare beams**
> **beyond which**
>
> **directly wait**
> **the night**

and day—

A profoundly refreshing emptiness pulsated at the core of it. This was the world, a world inside the world and so fully part of it, where the rocks vibrate, waterfalls are animate, visible objects harbor deposits of magical energy. Every instant of time is explosive, outrageous. Stillness is violent. It is the world and doesn't stand for some other thing.

It is work,

a large (or small) machine made of words

and here they are, a living dictionary finally. Whose words? Anybody's.

All that has been discarded, forgotten, walled off, left to rust or rot, or simply deposited in plain sight where anyone is free to ignore it, a world **oilgreen** and **drab** and **vinegar-smelling**, inescapable presence of **nozzle** and **slobber** and **drain-board**, **oozy fields** and **packed rifts**, **spongy greens** and **bitter horizontals**, landscape demarcated by **concrete disposal tank**— **withered weed stalks**—**cinder-bank**—**loose water-pipe**—**rubbish heap aflame**. To make a paradise out of debris, out of what is

> **broken—scorched—weathered—stained—shriveled— bent—dingy—scrawny—tawdry—festering—rank**

or by the same token from other sorts of debris, from

> **grandeur—solace—stateliness—finality—infinitely— ecstatic—glorified**

all being notes of the same music, banging against each other's echoes in junkyard gong tones.

Insisting, on the instant, if all else fails, by any means necessary—

> **Ha! poplars! teeth! May! wind! ringing! alive! lavender! come! poetry! breakfast! suddenly! This way ma'am! Let's have one! Say it!**

A place can be found for what a place must be found for, as if it were necessary to construct a rudimentary dwelling in order to write

Answer me
Talk to me
What can I say?
What have I to say to you
who are these people?
Forgive me
All I said was
I'm tired
I am ready for bed
I can't find time
I can't die

to find room even in the paradise of music for

Every familiar object is changed and dwarfed

or

In my life the furniture eats me

or

empty, windswept place

I carried the book around for several seasons of dissatisfaction and
confusion before accepting that there is never anything left to do but start,
by whatever means come to hand, tossing out or dropping in or simply
listening or making marks in the dark.

Begin, my friend,
for you cannot,
you may be sure,
take your song,
which drives all things out of mind,
with you to the other world.

34.

years later fragments of it continue to roll into the night

and I want to tell you right now everything that's going through my mind
                what is the use of talking, and there is no end of talking
                        allas, when shul my bones been at reste
my tong doth faile what I shuld crave
                this fals warld is bot transitory
                        pine boat a-shift on drift of tide
fall leaves fall die flowers away
                he has fled to the place where all lack a body
                        where will I be then who am now alone
I straddle my horse but there is no way back
                it runs a naked stream cold and chill
                        an icy wind blows from our stars
body my house my horse my hound
                I'm nothing, I'll always be nothing
                        I must have had it somewhere, somewhere here
this thing wings its way in
                slowly consumed like fire down a candle
                        stop killing the dead
you are an *I*
                yes, poetry ends like a rope
                        the end of an end is an echo
cars on the highway filled with speech
                because the string has broken for me
                        the roofy desert spreads vacant as Libya
far out the reefs lie naked
                far-folded mists
                        swaggering, shimmering fall
groves of enormous nameless flowers
                the painted cave of dream
                        a green thought in a green shade
I once more smell the dew and rain
                and only the narrow present is alive
                        without design or order or apparent action
dangling this way and that
                descends like a white mist into the court-yard
                        the inward gates of a bird are always open
in every part of every living thing
                the silken skilled transmemberment of song

hear her clear mirror
under the glassy cool translucent wave
till starlight disappears though the thing remain
broken music-footed ghost
sent out into a weather of doused torches
ghosts are here to listen
the rain waters the sentences
until breath wanders out of itself
at the point where I will disappear
some sun's growth beneath that holy star
there is a root deep in your brain that ties the sun to its gifts
the meadow more like a river than the river
when in the company of the gods I loved and was loved
the heart of thought, of the thought that brought them to be
the way air hides the sky
poetry is the great stimulation of life

SOURCES

1   "Diddle diddle dumpling"
    Traditional rhyme, existing in many variants

2   "Robin Hood"
    Theme song from *The Adventures of Robin Hood* (1955–60)
    Words and music by Carl Sigman (1909–2000)

3   "a little dab'll do ya"
    Excerpt from jingle for Bryllcreem, early 1950s; advertising agency, Kenyon & Eckhardt

4   "Where Go the Boats?"
    Robert Louis Stevenson, *A Child's Garden of Verses* (1885); issued by U.S. Camera Publishing Corporation (1944) with photographs by Toni Frissell

5   from "Jabberwocky"
    Lewis Carroll, *Through the Looking-Glass* (1871)

6   from "Danny Deever"
    Rudyard Kipling, *Barrack-Room Ballads and Other Verses* (1892)

7   Psalm 137, verses 1–5, King James Version

8   William Shakespeare, *A Midsummer Night's Dream* (c. 1596), excerpts from act 2, scene 1; as adapted for Classics Illustrated No. 87 (1951)

9   from *The Golden Apple* (1953), written by John Latouche, music by Jerome Moross
    On the original cast recording (RCA Victor, 1954), the song is sung by Jack Whiting

10 from "The City in the Sea"
    Edgar Allan Poe, *The Raven and Other Poems* (1845); *The Poetry of Edgar Allan Poe*, Heritage Press (1943), with lithographs by Hugo Steiner-Prag

11 William Shakespeare, *Macbeth* (c. 1606), excerpts from act 1, scene 5
    Pamela Brown played Lady Macbeth on the RCA Victor release LM 6010 (1953), with Alec Guinness as Macbeth
    The Classics Illustrated adaptation (No. 128) of *Macbeth* was published in 1955

12 from *Salome* (1891)
    Oscar Wilde, translated from the French by Lord Alfred Douglas
    The Heritage Press (1945), illustrated by Valenti Angelo with introduction by Holbrook Jackson

13 from *Philoctetes* (c. 409 BC)
Sophocles; translated by David Grene; *The Complete Greek Tragedies* (University of Chicago Press, 1957)

14 "Departure"
Wang Wei (699–761); translated by Robert Payne and others; title supplied by translator; collected in John D. Yohannan, *A Treasury of Asian Literature* (John Day Company, 1956)

15 *The Rubáiyát of Omar Khayyám*, stanza 46
Omar Khayyám (1048–1141), translated by Edward Fitzgerald; first edition, 1859
The Heritage Press (1946), with illustrations by Arthur Szyk

16 from "Thirteen Ways of Looking at a Blackbird"
Wallace Stevens, *Harmonium*, 1923; anthologized in Conrad Aiken, *Modern American Poets*, The Modern Library, 1927

17 from *Kantan*
Attributed to Zeami Motokiyo (1363–1444); translated by Arthur Waley in *The Nō Plays of Japan*, 1921; reprinted by Grove Press, 1957
"A book with a photograph of the mask": P. G. O'Neill, *A Guide to Nō*, Tokyo: Hinoki Shoten, 1953

18 "The flowers withered"
Ono no Komachi, from the first Imperial anthology *Kokinshū* (905); translated by Donald Keene in his *Anthology of Japanese Literature*, Grove Press, 1955
The lines from *Sotoba Komachi* are from Arthur Waley's *The Nō Plays of Japan*, cited above
"Full many a flower": Thomas Gray, *Elegy Written in a Country Churchyard* (1751)

19 from "I Cover the Waterfront" (1933)
Lyrics by Edward Heyman; music by Johnny Green
Recorded on multiple occasions by Billie Holiday (1944 and subsequently)

20 from "Howl"
Allen Ginsberg, *Howl and Other Poems*, City Lights Books, 1956

21 "When I Heard the Learn'd Astronomer"
Walt Whitman, *Leaves of Grass*, 1891–92; first published in *Drum-Taps*, 1865; anthologized in F. O. Matthiessen, *The Oxford Book of American Verse*, 1950

22 from *The Metamorphoses*, Book I
Ovid (43 BC–c. 18 AD), translated by Horace Gregory; Viking Press, 1958

23 "Claude Allen"
Date of composition between 1913 and 1918; as performed by Clarence Ashley
(1895–1967) on *Old-Time Music at Clarence Ashley's*, Folkways Records, 1961

24 from "Benares Song"
The Rise and Fall of the City of Mahagonny (1930) by Bertolt Brecht and Kurt Weill;
Lotte Lenya sang the role of Jenny on the Columbia release K3L 243 (1956)
The words of "Benares Song" have been attributed to Brecht but are now credited to
Elisabeth Hauptmann
Japanese in Thirty Hours by Eiichi Kyooka (Tokyo: The Hokuseido Press, 1942;
revised edition 1951)

25 *Jungle Moon Men*
Film (1955) directed by Charles S. Gould, written by Jo Pagano and Dwight
V. Babcock, and starring Johnny Weissmuller and Helene Stanton; released by
Columbia Pictures

26 from *Bleak House*
Charles Dickens, 1853
Also: Joseph Conrad, *Nostromo*, 1904; Nathaniel Hawthorne, *The Marble Faun*, 1860;
Herman Melville, *Moby Dick*, 1851; William Faulkner, *Pylon*, 1935

27 "He is more than a hero" (excerpt)
Sappho; translated by Mary Barnard in *Sappho: A New Translation*, University of
California Press, 1958

28 from "Kubla Khan"
Samuel Taylor Coleridge; written 1797; first published as "Kubla Khan: Or, A Vision
in a Dream" in *Christabel: Kubla Khan, A Vision; The Pains of Sleep* (1816)

29 "Rose-cheek'd Laura, come"
Thomas Campion, from *Observations in the Art of English Poesy* (1602)
"weep you no more": music by John Dowland; "the silver swan": music by Orland
Gibbons; "I saw my lady weep": music by John Dowland; "I must go walk the wood
so wild": author unknown; "are those clear fires that vanish into smoke": "Can
She Excuse My Wrongs," music by John Dowland; "follow thy fair sun unhappy
shadow": Thomas Campion, from *A Book of Ayres* (1601); "like melting snow": Ben
Jonson, "Slow, slow, fresh fount" from *Cynthia's Revels* (1600)

30 from "Elegy 19: To His Mistris Going To Bed"
John Donne, date of composition unknown, first published 1633
"where shadows do for bodies stand": "Can She Excuse My Wrongs," author
unknown, music by John Dowland; "are they shadows that we see": Samuel Daniel,
"Song" from *Tethys' Festival* (1610); "makes both one": John Donne, "The Extasie";

"All here in one bed lay": John Donne, "The Sunne Rising"; "Let sea-discoverers to new worlds": John Donne, "The Good-Morrow"

31 from "Auguries of Innocence" (c. 1803)
    William Blake
    "his accepted brethren"; "And the just man rages"; "Sooner murder an infant"; "Body is a portion of the Soul": *The Marriage of Heaven and Hell* (c. 1790), collected in *Blake: The Laurel Poetry Series*, edited by Richard Wilbur with an introduction by Ruthven Todd, Dell, 1960.

32 from "Childhood" (part 5)
    Arthur Rimbaud, *Illuminations* (written c. 1871–75, published 1886); translated by Louise Varèse (New Directions, 1946)

33 from "Perpetuum Mobile: The City"
    Adam and Eve and the City (1936), included in William Carlos Williams, *The Collected Earlier Poems* (New Directions, 1951)
    "A poem is a small (or large) machine": from Author's Introduction to *The Wedge* (1944), included in William Carlos Williams, *The Collected Later Poems* (New Directions, 1963)
    "Begin, my friend": from "Theocritus: Idyl I" in William Carlos Williams, *The Desert Music and Other Poems* (Random House, 1954)
    It was Louise Landes Levi who encouraged me to read Snyder and Williams, at some point in the mid-1960s.

34 Lines and phrases from Otis Redding; Li Po/Ezra Pound; Geoffrey Chaucer; Thomas Wyatt; William Dunbar; Confucian Odes/Ezra Pound; Emily Brontë; William Carlos Williams; Robert Creeley; Li Ho/A. C. Graham; John Clare; Georg Trakl/Michael Hamburger; May Swenson; Fernando Pessoa/Richard Zenith; William Bronk; John Wieners; Han Shan/Gary Snyder; Giuseppe Ungaretti/Allen Ginsberg; Elizabeth Bishop; Jack Spicer; Laura Riding; George Oppen; Día!kwain; Herman Melville; Trumbull Stickney; Alfred Tennyson; Basil Bunting; Robert Hayden; Muriel Rukeyser; Andrew Marvell; George Herbert; Charles Reznikoff; Emily Dickinson; Henry David Thoreau; Langston Hughes; Hugh MacDiarmid; Lorine Niedecker; Hart Crane; Louis Zukofsky; John Milton; Eliot Weinberger; Nathaniel Mackey; Albert Mobilio; Dino Campana/Charles Wright; Elaine Equi; August Kleinzahler; Pierre Reverdy; Amiri Baraka; Mark Kirschen; Michael O'Brien; H.D.; Joseph Donahue; John Ashbery; Susan Howe

TITLES FROM MARSH HAWK PRESS

Jane Augustine *Arbor Vitae; Krazy; Night Lights; A Woman's Guide to Mountain Climbing*

Tom Beckett *Dipstick (Diptych)*

Sigman Byrd *Under the Wanderer's Star*

Patricia Carlin *Original Green; Quantum Jitters; Second Nature*

Claudia Carlson *The Elephant House; My Chocolate Sarcophagus; Pocket Park*

Meredith Cole *Miniatures*

Jon Curley *Hybrid Moments; Scorch Marks*

Neil de la Flor *Almost Dorothy; An Elephant's Memory of Blizzards*

Chard deNiord *Sharp Golden Thorn*

Sharon Dolin *Serious Pink*

Steve Fellner *Blind Date with Cavafy; The Weary World Rejoices*

Thomas Fink *Selected Poems & Poetic Series; Joyride; Peace Conference; Clarity and Other Poems; After Taxes; Gossip*

Thomas Fink and Maya D. Mason *A Pageant for Every Addiction*

Norman Finkelstein *Inside the Ghost Factory; Passing Over*

Edward Foster *The Beginning of Sorrows; Dire Straits; Mahrem: Things Men Should Do for Men; Sewing the Wind; What He Ought to Know*

Paolo Javier *The Feeling is Actual*

Burt Kimmelman *Abandoned Angel; Somehow*

Burt Kimmelman and Fred Caruso *The Pond at Cape May Point*

Basil King *77 Beasts; Disparate Beasts; Mirage; The Spoken Word / The Painted Hand from Learning to Draw / A History*

Martha King *Imperfect Fit*

Phillip Lopate *At the End of the Day: Selected Poems and An Introductory Essay*

Mary Mackey *Breaking the Fever; The Jaguars That Prowl Our Dreams; Sugar Zone; Travelers With No Ticket Home*

Jason McCall *Dear Hero,*

Sandy McIntosh *The After-Death History of My Mother; Between Earth and Sky; Cemetery Chess; Ernesta, in the Style of the Flamenco; Forty-Nine Guaranteed Ways to Escape Death; A Hole In the Ocean; Lesser Lights; Obsessional*

Stephen Paul Miller *Any Lie You Tell Will Be the Truth; The Bee Flies in May; Fort Dad; Skinny Eighth Avenue; There's Only One God and You're Not It*

Daniel Morris *Blue Poles; Bryce Passage; Hit Play; If Not for the Courage*

Gail Newman *Blood Memory*

Geoffrey O'Brien *The Blue Hill*

Sharon Olinka *The Good City*

Christina Olivares *No Map of the Earth Includes Stars*

Justin Petropoulos *Eminent Domain*

Paul Pines *Charlotte Songs; Divine Madness; Gathering Sparks; Last Call at the Tin Palace*

Jacquelyn Pope *Watermark*

George Quasha *Things Done for Themselves*

Karin Randolph *Either She Was*

Rochelle Ratner *Balancing Acts; Ben Casey Days; House and Home*

Michael Rerick *In Ways Impossible to Fold*

Corrine Robins *Facing It; One Thousand Years; Today's Menu*

Eileen R. Tabios *The Connoisseur of Alleys; I Take Thee, English, for My Beloved; The In(ter)vention of the Hay(na)ku; The Light Sang as It Left Your Eyes; Reproductions of the Empty Flagpole; Sun Stigmata; The Thorn Rosary*

Eileen R. Tabios and j/j hastain *The Relational Elations of Orphaned Algebra*

Susan Terris *Familiar Tense; Ghost of Yesterday; Natural Defenses*

Lynne Thompson *Fretwork*

Madeline Tiger *Birds of Sorrow and Joy*

Tana Jean Welch *Latest Volcano*

Harriet Zinnes *Drawing on the Wall; Light Light or the Curvature of the Earth; New and Selected Poems; Weather is Whether; Whither Nonstopping*

YEAR	AUTHOR	MHP POETRY PRIZE TITLE	JUDGE
2004	Jacquelyn Pope	*Watermark*	Marie Ponsot
2005	Sigman Byrd	*Under the Wanderer's Star*	Gerald Stern
2006	Steve Fellner	*Blind Date with Cavafy*	Denise Duhamel
2007	Karin Randolph	*Either She Was*	David Shapiro
2008	Michael Rerick	*In Ways Impossible to Fold*	Thylias Moss
2009	Neil de la Flor	*Almost Dorothy*	Forrest Gander
2010	Justin Petropoulos	*Eminent Domain*	Anne Waldman
2011	Meredith Cole	*Miniatures*	Alicia Ostriker
2012	Jason McCall	*Dear Hero,*	Cornelius Eady
2013	Tom Beckett	*Dipstick (Diptych)*	Charles Bernstein
2014	Christina Olivares	*No Map of the Earth Includes Stars*	Brenda Hillman
2015	Tana Jean Welch	*Latest Volcano*	Stephanie Strickland
2016	Robert Gibb	*After*	Mark Doty
2017	Geoffrey O'Brien	*The Blue Hill*	Meena Alexander
2018	Lynne Thompson	*Fretwork*	Jane Hirshfield
2019	Gail Newman	*Blood Memory*	Marge Piercy

ARTISTIC ADVISORY BOARD

For more information, please go to: **www.marshhawkpress.org**